Paul V. Marshall

Same-Sex Unions

Unions

Stories and Rites

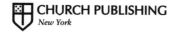

CHURCH PUBLISHING
New York

A catalog record for this book is available from
the Library of Congress

ISBN 0-89869-417-5

Church Publishing Incorporated
445 Fifth Avenue
New York, NY 10016
www.churchpublishing.org

5 4 3 2 1

Same-Sex
Unions

Contents

Part Three
LITURGIES

Part Four
HEARING TEST:
SERMONS

Introductory Note

An early version of this study arose as I tried to prepare myself for discussion with colleagues in the months before the 2003 General Convention of the Episcopal Church, which was due to discuss same-sex blessings.[1] It was shared in self-published form with fellow bishops and some other members of the Convention so that discussion about same-sex blessings would have a bit of noncontentious context, and that we could discuss information rather than attitude.

Despite assertions to the contrary, the General Convention did not endorse, set out, or provide for trial use rites for blessing same-sex unions. It declined to ask the Standing Commission on Liturgy and Music to conduct further explorations in the area.

It did do two things, however. First, it asked the Presiding Bishop to bring before the church materials it might study before taking up the question again. Second, it declined to disfellowship or excommunicate those communities (perhaps most famously, the Diocese of New Westminster, Vancouver, Canada, or our own diocese in Delaware) that feel led to work on and experience the use of rites for same-sex couples. The legislation recognizes them, despite the controversial nature of their actions, to be living "within the bounds of our communion."

In the early summer of 2004, it appears that several more dioceses will be shortly producing rites for communities (usually parishes) to use in blessing same-sex unions. A considerable number of parish communities are acting within the provisions of the

---

1. I should point out at the very beginning that because the liturgies being proposed in the Episcopal Church in general and particularly in the Claiming the Blessing movement usually use the expression "same-sex" rather than "same-gender," I follow that usage throughout.

convention resolution. Thus, the discussion of these liturgies is here to stay, and thus I have agreed with the request of Church Publishing to enlarge my original work and share it in a larger arena as a contribution to what promises to be a lengthy conversation. I have two goals here, as reflected in the subtitle of this book, *Stories and Rites*. The first is to keep the promise made at the 1998 Lambeth Conference and listen carefully and fraternally to the stories of gay and lesbian believers, honestly and without judgment — to understand their life and witness on their terms. The second is to review what is happening *liturgically* as communities attempt to shape rites.

I have tried to listen to stories as accurately as I could and have presented them in a way that those whom I interviewed have agreed represents what they have to say. I have tried to bring whatever skills I have as a professional in liturgical studies to an objective and detailed analysis of the rites mentioned below. However, disclosure is appropriate here. It is no secret how any deputy or bishop voted at the General Convention in 2003, either on the consecration of the Bishop of New Hampshire or the legislation regarding unions, and I voted with the majority in both cases. I should also state my identity as the sole author of the resolution language indicating that those who work with or celebrate unions in this time of study and exploration are operating "within the bounds of our communion." This was done both to moderate the entirely negative language of the resolution and to allow room for the Holy Spirit to teach the church. Readers will make whatever they will out of those facts, but they should be on the table in assessing the objectivity of the liturgical analysis in this study.

There is a sense in which the question has changed a good deal in the little less than a year since General Convention acted. The Commonwealth of Massachusetts began uniting same-sex couples in marriages that have legal parity with opposite-sex marriages. What is happening in the secular realm has both everything and nothing to do with the question before the church. It has nothing to do with what is before the church in the sense that what the state does in the American legal system does not bind the church's thinking about the nature of relationships in the divine order, and no member of the clergy is obliged to act for the state in any marriage at all. It has everything to do with what is before us because in the Bay State, at least, there are couples whom the law recognizes as married who are asking the church to witness and bless their union in precisely the same sense that any other couple would seek a blessing of a previously conducted civil marriage. The Diocese of Vermont has already responded in careful detail to the provision in that state for civil unions. The discussion is no longer hypothetical on any plane, a fact that underscores the need to analyze the situation dispassionately.

Part One

STORIES

In Mary Tanner's address to the Anglican Society entitled "The Future of the Anglican Communion," the noted Church of England ecumenist repeats one of the concerns of this book with admirable precision. After observing that the Communion has failed to do its theological homework on a broad basis, she adds

> Nor have we begun together to listen to the experience of homosexual persons as the Lambeth resolution calls for. When all are invited to the table, and encouraged to name themselves honestly and openly, the discussion becomes not one about outsiders but a conversation about us and our life together. It becomes "our issue" in a new way. History does not lead us to believe that God never does a new thing, or that God is not at work in the world ahead of us.[1]

Tanner also quotes Stephen Cottrell's observation that "there is always the tendency to replace the risky freedom of relationship with God with the controlling safety of a religious system, where some are counted in while others are excluded."

The obligation simply to listen is one I take with great seriousness, as my own experience in all aspects of life is that issues change when there are faces attached to them, when we have walked a bit in the other's moccasins. A more academic way to state this

---

1. The speech is reproduced in its entirety in *The Anglican* (July 2004): 10–18.

principle is that data and concepts cannot be considered without a context when human beings are involved. Accordingly, it is a matter of great regret that the obligation accepted by the bishops at Lambeth was quietly laid aside. As a microscopic gesture of atonement for this situation I report in this section on visits with two couples, one lesbian and one gay. It is more than justice that motivates me, however, because like all theological problems, liturgical questions are not abstract. They are pastoral and communal, and must be addressed as such. I hope that if the reader and I together meet these four people, the rest of what we study together will have a pastoral context. This is not to say that knowing the people answers all questions facing the church, but it is to assert that how they are answered will change.

The two couples represent different generations; Bob and Charles are "Reliables" born before 1945, and Brenda and Anne are members of the much-discussed "Gen X." The couples have taken different paths in their life as partners. Anne and Brenda very much wanted a liturgical moment that they consider a wedding, while Bob and Charles do not use the language of marriage at all and have not had the desire for a liturgical rite cementing their union. Brenda and Anne enjoy the energetic life of the city while Charles and Bob are drawn to quiet life in a rural setting. Anne and Brenda have a child while Bob and Charles do not (they do have godchildren). What I relate concerning Charles and Bob is briefer than the account of Brenda and Anne because there is no liturgy on which to report; I nonetheless hope that I have given them adequate representation.

The goal was to listen to a male couple and to a female couple who were church people and in long-term relationships. It turned out for all four individuals that it was a church relationship that was a significant part of their personal integration. It is an accident that each couple is composed of people who came to the Episcopal Church from other traditions, yet that accident is itself data with which we must deal in a time when the growth of the church is very much in our awareness.

As a way to test whether I am hearing gay and lesbian Episcopalians correctly, I have placed at the very end of this book two sermons I preached in the early summer of 2004 at liturgies where these concerns were paramount. I would be interested to know from gay and lesbian readers whether I have heard them correctly (bishop@diobeth.org).

Chapter One

Anne and Brenda

A nne and Brenda Bost live with their five-year-old son, Henry, in a traditionally and cheerfully decorated apartment near the heart of Greenwich Village, in the pleasant kind of building where the door attendant smiles at, greets, and announces the visitor. The Bost family can walk to their church and Henry's school through a neighborhood that is both quaint and intense.

It was not always this way. Until late in 2001 they lived in New York's financial district. The disaster of September 11 of that year forced them, like thousands of others, out of their home for three months. The trauma of the cataclysm next door made it terribly difficult for their son to return to that apartment, so ultimately they moved north. For much of their time away from their downtown home they lived as refugees at the General Theological Seminary, several neighborhoods uptown in Chelsea. In addition to the seminary community, the supportive and stabilizing element in this terrible time was their parish church, St. Luke in the Fields, where liturgical fellowship, corporate pastoral care, and uncommon helpfulness gave them spiritual and emotional gifts that they still cherish.

Anne is an attorney, and Brenda is a nurse. Each is from the South. Anne is winsome and voluble, Brenda a bit more reserved but always careful to be accurate and effective in what she says. Each impresses one with the dignity that only thoroughly examined lives radiate. They have been together for eleven years, and some six years ago adopted a common surname when Brenda also adopted the son Anne had borne. Watching them in action with their slightly rambunctious kindergartner (with that behavioral edge added, on the day I visited them, by a New York kid's *de rigueur* ear infection), brought to mind only that these were two committed parents slightly embarrassed by their offspring but not about to quit raising him with patience and love. They have been and are a family in every sense.

Why then, ten years into their relationship, in September of 2002, did they mark their commitment to each other in a liturgical celebration? Part of the answer lies in what religion had come to mean for them. Although their religious backgrounds were in different denominations, each learned rejection and condemnation of same-sex relationships as a part of Christian religion. Neither was impressed by the argument that one could intensely *hate* an act or state of being and still claim to love the one whose act or state it was, and religion accordingly receded in their awareness for some years.

Anne and Brenda report rediscovering the power of God and the dynamic of the church in the formation course they took in preparation for reception into the Episcopal Church. In that course they also fell in love with the deuterocanonical book of Wisdom, which was to provide the keynote in the liturgy of the word at their celebration. The decision to celebrate their covenant publicly was inseparable from the decision to do so at St. Luke's, where Anne is now a member of the vestry. It was to be at St. Luke's and not some more fashionable or hip place, she said without further elaboration, "because that's our home."

At the same time, they recognize that the planning and celebration of this liturgy "was a part of the evolution of St. Luke's." The parish had already been the site for what they considered "second-class, secret services in the [parish's] Garden." They were not interested in having an ambiguous "service about friendship," as Anne put it, and chose to wait until a complete liturgy was possible. When I asked, given that this was an evolutionary moment for a church on Christopher Street in Greenwich Village, if they could appreciate that the evolutionary journey might be a longer one in other parts of the country, their answer was not defensive. "We weren't very threatening," was their reply, as the parish already knew them from long-term commitment and had seen them through the terrible time of the 9/11 apocalypse. The preparation and celebration were about an "us," not about some theoretical pair of lesbians, and came quite easily to the parish community.

Although the rector of the parish (who was on sabbatical as all this was taking shape) later thanked them for their "bravery" and the "ministry" they had done by being the first in the parish to go through the preparation and celebration of a complete rite, they had not for the most part seen their service in a heroic light. The decision at St. Luke's that it was time to move to public celebration was not made by parish resolution, opinion poll, or referendum, but pastorally. There were no secrets about it, but it was understood as a personal and sacramental matter rather than an act of revolution.

The curate and the parish deacon worked with Anne and Brenda in preparing the liturgy and in the preservice counseling. The curate reinforced their instinct to avoid the "second class" by insisting that all the ritual actions present in an opposite-sex wedding be part of Anne and Brenda's liturgy. For example, St. Luke's is a bit remarkable in that it retains the custom of binding the hands of the newly married couple with the celebrant's stole, but that is what it does, and so the priest built that act into the rite planned for Anne and Brenda. Essentially, the look and feel of celebrating covenanted life-commitment was to be the same regardless of the parties. (The binding of the hands, although not with a stole, is suggested in the liturgy of the Consultation on Same-Sex Unions.)

As would any other couple, Anne and Brenda had to meet St. Luke's prenuptial requirements: a year of regular church attendance and maintenance of a pledge (in addition to the marriage service's rubrical requirement of baptism). Above all, they were required to meet with clergy for counseling. The deacon led them through this process. As with most couples, they were not sure what to expect, but discovered that there was more to this idea of couple counseling than the intensely personal focus of psychotherapy. They were asked to focus on the relating, the relationship that was a third entity in their lives. Like many couples, they discovered similarities of outlook and belief to a greater extent than they had realized, and explored growing edges as well. The most impressive thing about their discussion of their counseling was how valuable yet unremarkable it all was.

The planning of the liturgy took a great deal of care, since it was close to the Prayer Book but also needed to be different because of who the "brides" (as they put it) were. Their reference to "brides" was intentional, because the first point in conceiving the liturgy was that it look not like somebody was "the man," as Brenda put it, but that it be about two women and look like it. Thus each would be escorted down the aisle, one by Anne's father and the other by Henry, and they would also trade escorts at the altar. Each would carry flowers.

For the liturgy itself, they made two decisions negatively. They had attended quite a few rites that had been expressed in the tactful language of friendship: at every decision point in the planning, according to Anne, they thought back on these encounters and "did the opposite." Unlike the planners of many same-sex rites, they entirely eliminated the "Dearly Beloved" part of the traditional service rather than replace it with something that might be tendentious, awkward, or stilted. There was also no inquiry into the existence of impediments to the union, as there are no civil or ecclesiastical laws to apply in New York. Instead, after the procession, the Eucharist began as usual, with the ordinary chants sung to Monteverdi's solid but ethereal *Missa in illo tempore*. This was to be Church, and no mistake about it.

The Collect of the Day was based on the Collect found at the same point in the Prayer Book service, with its use of the language of covenant, but also with the deliciously provocative notion that God might be enjoying this party:

O gracious and everliving God, look joyfully upon Anne and
Brenda, who come before this community to make a covenant
of love, fidelity, and lifelong commitment. Grant them your blessing and assist them with your grace, that, with true fidelity and
steadfast love, they may honor and keep the covenant they make,
though Jesus Christ. . . .

The first lesson was from Wisdom, the couple's signature
scripture. The passage (8:9–16) begins,

Therefore I determined to take her to live with me, knowing that
she would give me good counsel and encouragement in cares and
grief. Because of her I shall have glory among the multitudes and
honor in the presence of the elders, though I am young.

Then would come an anthem, the familiar "entreat me not
to leave thee," of the Ruth and Naomi story, but in the delicate
vigor of a setting by Heinrich Schütz. The Epistle was the "love
chapter," of 1 Corinthians, and the Gospel the Matthean form
of the Beatitudes. The deacon who had prepared the couple then
preached.

The section following the sermon in the Prayer Book is called
"The Marriage," followed by a section called "The Blessing of the
Marriage." In Anne and Brenda's service these are collapsed into
a large section called "The Covenant and Blessing." This section
contains all of the elements of the Prayer Book service: vows, rings,
prayers, and blessing. It also adds the elements of sponsorship by
the entire community (there is only one small question about support for the couple in the "Dearly Beloved" section of the Prayer
Book rite). Both services follow the Blessing of the Couple with the
exchange of the Peace. Anne describes this section as having gone
through very many drafts and much discussion between couple
and clergy until the right balance was found.

As we shall see, in predecessor rites for same-sex blessings there
is a bit more interrogation before the covenanting, and more emphasis is placed on communal support. This reflects an awareness
that couples not in the heterosexual majority seldom get sufficient

support from the community at large. Thus the couple stand before the celebrant, who asks a question that has appeared in many initiatory liturgies throughout the years: "What do you seek?" They answer, "We ask a blessing from this community on our covenant," and one notes the assignment of the role of blessing to the community rather than the priest or the church at large, possibly an acknowledgment that the immediate community has a significant stake in the couple's success, and certainly an indication that in an uncertain time communal validation is no small thing.

Before addressing the assembly with the question about its support, which is stated so simply (and perhaps perfunctorily) in the Prayer Book marriage rite, the celebrant here is specific and blunt:

> Will you, brothers and sisters in Christ, give your pledge to honor and uphold Anne and Brenda, to recognize them as a family in this community, to guide and pray for them in times of trouble, to celebrate with them in times of joy, to respect the bonds of their covenant, and to seek to discern the continuing presence of Christ within them?

The community is asked for recognition and support — and also to respect boundaries, reflecting wisdom gathered from the lives of couples of any composition.

What kind of vows would a lawyer write? What kind would a nurse write? There are familiar concepts but interesting textual divergences of emphasis in the vows Anne and Brenda wrote. They include what is promised by those using the Prayer Book marriage service, but in fact they seem to promise more:

> In the name of God and before this congregation, I, N., promise you, N., to honor and cherish you, to share with you in life's joys and triumphs, and to stand with you in times of grief and misfortune. I will be truthful in all things and strive with you to create a home filled with reverence and hospitality. I promise to love you all the days of my life. This is my solemn vow.

To the ordinary promise of lifelong fidelity through good and ill fortune, Anne and Brenda have added the elements of truthfulness, reverence, and hospitality, all reflective of their readings in the wisdom traditions.

The rings were blessed in the usual way and exchanged with words not much different from those of the Prayer Book, but with additional terms of endearment, "I give you this ring as a symbol of my vow to you, my friend, my sister, my partner, my spouse." Gone, however, is the expression "with all that I have and all that I am, I honor you," our flaccid and puritan circumlocution for 1662's robust "with my body I thee worship, and with all my worldly goods I thee endow." When I asked why there was not a parallel formula in their rite, Anne said that it just had not come up in discussion.

The prayers are the first half of those of the marriage service with very slight and occasional adaptation, such as replacing "marriage" with "lifelong covenant." The prayers conclude with the final petitions of Form IV of the Prayers of the People in the Rite Two Eucharist. The prayers were chanted by Anne's father.

The blessing is based on the second form provided in the Prayer Book rite, with the first line altered to speak of covenants rather than marriage, and to avoid the spousal language used regarding Christ and the church.

There followed the Peace, and the Eucharist was celebrated. The offertory was a version of Bach's "Jesu, Joy of Man's Desiring," in a translation that echoed the first lesson with the reference to Christ as "holy wisdom." The Proper Preface was that of the Ascension, and the Communion Motet was William Byrd's "O sacrum convivium."

The classical and slightly abstracted element in the music was balanced by the preservice music, a jazz improvisation on Beethoven's "Hymn to Joy," by New Orleans musical figure David Ellington. The postlude was on the fun side, a seventeenth-century battle song chosen in part so that Henry could hear the bells of the organ's Zimbelstern, his favorite stop.

The choices in service music and of an elaborate liturgy that demanded much of the participants conveyed Anne and Brenda's taste, to be sure, but they also conveyed their intention that this liturgy be fully that of their parish church, celebrated with fullest integrity.

They also know a thing or two about parties, and the festivities continued very publicly. The entire assembly, about 110 people, marched through Greenwich Village as though it were a village in France or Italy. Photographs reveal the onlookers getting up from sidewalk cafes to make way, cheering the couple and their friends as they moved through their village. What followed was in the New Orleans tradition, and thus was not a reception, but well and truly a party of major proportions. The photographs suggest that even the photographer got into the mood of the event.

Anne and Brenda consistently refer to this event as "our wedding" and were emphatic in telling me that use of this expression was "not political," but simply describes "what it is." We will want to pay attention to this observation in the next chapter. Anne says that she never "worried about offending people," because she and Brenda were acting with integrity with no intent to "get into anyone's face." Brenda was characteristically direct: when speaking of her desire that the rite be clearly that for two women, she summed up with "this was the right thing...I wanted to stand before the community" as who and what she was.

After we had gotten through the discussion of their previous life and the liturgical celebration, I asked what I believed to be a crucial question: How, if at all, was their life together different now that they had been through this celebration? I had to ask each of them separately, as they were by this time taking turns with Henry in another room, so the convergence of their answers is striking. Anne said that they were both a bit surprised to find that the entire event was "more than a rubber stamp or a big party." She was "surprised, after a long relationship, how renewed and blessed" they felt. She had a new perception of how supported their life is — and how their commitment deepened accordingly.

Brenda's thoughts were similar. "Getting married — I felt very blessed. It really became part of my shield." She then spoke of the importance of community support, but took me a bit by surprise when she added, "Now I'm looking at ways that I can give back." In thirty-two years of ordained ministry I had never heard anyone respond to a marriage service this way, so I asked her to talk about that some more. "It took this," meaning the union service, for her to become thoroughly enthused about community, specifically that of the church. But far beyond that, she reports a heightened desire to help gay and lesbian families make intergenerational connections. She and Anne have in fact sponsored an intergenerational picnic as part of Gay Pride observances, and she feels an intensified commitment to that, but also speaks of it now with the word "ministry."

Brenda can also speak of the last several years as being a healing experience for her. When I asked Brenda directly if she would speak of the development of the relationship with Anne and particularly of the liturgy at St. Luke's as being a part of her salvation, she readily agreed, adding that it was a "big part." She said that, whereas previously "I didn't feel safe anywhere," she has come to know the meaning of healing, community, and family with Anne and at St. Luke's. There is a peculiar note of conviction in her voice when she says of Henry and St. Luke's that "he was born out of that place."

Chapter Two

Charles and Bob

U nlike Brenda and Anne, Charles Rice and Bob Barker live quietly in near-seclusion on ample acreage in the Pocono Mountains. Three dogs and a cat live with them in their farmhouse. A long-term friend occupies the bottom floor of the German bank barn that serves as guest house and social area. There is a charming gazebo by the little lake at the center of their property. The visitor is impressed by the peacefulness of it all, and by the evident love of gardening, books, and everything visual — all things bright and beautiful, but nothing hurried, fussy, or loud. If there is a television in either building, I did not see it. There is space, light, and quiet. The visitor wants to stay, and the hospitality offered is gracious and natural. The week before I last visited them, HGTV had spent the day filming their home.

Their place reflects the sensibilities and histories of its inhabitants. Charles is a retired professor and still serves as a priest and teacher. Bob is a graphic designer in his own firm and is increasingly interested in interior design. He is also senior warden in his parish church. Both are quiet and reflective, gentle and free of anxiety. Their stories converged at about the same time in life as did Anne and Brenda's, but they have now been together for twenty-nine years.

Charles was born on a farm in Oklahoma before the Second World War and is partially Cherokee in ancestry. He attended Baylor University and began serving Baptist churches at the age of twenty. Somewhat later he attended the Baptist seminary in Louisville, where his principal area of interest was New Testament, and where he was president of the student body. Encouraged by a mentor, he then went to Union Theological Seminary in New York, where he studied with the leading teacher of preaching in his day. From Union he went to Duke, where he taught preaching and was dean of students while earning his Ph.D. in religion and culture.

Charles went to Africa as a missionary and teacher for the United Church of Christ and taught with Desmond Tutu. Finally, Charles moved to Drew University in New Jersey, where he taught preaching for over thirty years. He has served for many years on the board of the Kirkridge Retreat and Study Center and continues to teach for that center. His work in spirituality and literature is highly regarded.

Charles has made seven pilgrimages to Taizé, staying for a month the first time. While he was very interested in what that community was doing, he confesses that he "didn't go to have my life changed," but that is what happened nonetheless. Immersed in prayer and liturgy, he found his spirituality formed in a new way. Back in New Jersey after his first visit to Taizé, the change crystallized on a Sunday morning when he was preaching in an Episcopal parish. Dressed in his black U.C.C. preaching gown, he was assisting with the chalice when, while he was already some-what overwhelmed with what he was doing, "a black lady looked up as with a face that seemed to ask, 'Who the hell are you?' " The sense that he needed to identify outwardly with the sacramental tradition into which his soul had moved became irresistible at that moment. Back at the altar he whispered to the celebrant, "I just joined the Episcopal Church." He acted on that realization and was eventually ordained by the Bishop John Spong of Newark.

Being a gay man raised as a Southern Baptist was, as he modestly puts it, "a burden." Sexuality was not generally dis-cussed in his childhood home. There was certainly no reference to homosexuality, except for one oblique reference to "funny men." Charles was successful at pleasing adults, and at church he had many friends and supporters. His devotion and giftedness made

him the darling of people who supported him throughout his edu-
cation, and there was accordingly strong pressure on him to keep
his identity hidden. His instincts were justified when his principal
friends and supporters cut him off entirely when they learned of his
sexuality. During his student days his self-esteem was not aided by
the academic and theological writers of the 1950s, and he remem-
bers with some present pain what it felt like to read about people
like himself in books that added the language of disease along to
that of sin, intensifying the loathsome picture of homosexuality
that his culture bore.

Charles experienced transformation spiritually when he confronted his sexuality with a compassionate pastor. Late at night,
burdened by anxiety, he poured out his agonies to this colleague,
who listened to the whole tale and simply said, "Well, Charles,
you know, if you find that the Lord has given you a wooden leg,
you're just going to have to learn to dance with it." The idea that
he was *entitled* to dance, he says, has allowed him to live from
that moment "without guilt or self-doubt or loathing." When I
responded that it sounded like conservative Christians were ironi-
cally right in insisting that encountering Christ does indeed change
gay people, although in a way conservatives would not predict, he
replied, "You can quote me on that."

Charles reports that his family has come to accept him for who
is. He met Bob in 1975, and the family now affirms their relationship, although this was a gradual process. However, unlike Brenda,
he experienced no family condemnation of who he was, although
there was a strained period of a year when he first came completely
out about his relationship. Charles pointed out the difference for
parents between what is tacitly understood ("all mothers know,"
he observed) and what is acknowledged publicly. He agreed that
the situation families face is very much like that confronting the
church in the matter of gay clergy: church people have always
known, but public acknowledgment is a more challenging issue.

Bob grew up a fundamentalist in New Jersey, the son of a
lay preacher who died when Bob was sixteen. His family was

uniformly devout and he "lived in the church world." When he realized that he was different and that his difference was unacceptable in the church's eyes, his estrangement from religion grew, and he left that world. He dealt with the church's rejection of him by "not thinking about church for twenty-five years — there is no point thinking about it when they will just condemn."

Bob describes his coming out as slow, taking place only in his twenties. His entry into gay life came through counseling with a Lutheran minister while Bob was a student at the Pratt Institute in New York. His experience was less tortured than that of Charles because he found himself making a rational decision based on his assessment of who he was — without church in the picture. Thus, although he took his time about it, he "never had a second of guilt about being gay — it was just me." Religion as he knew it, however, could not be a part of who he was, and he believes that his experience in this regard is not at all uncommon.

He began his career in the world of print with Fortress Press, did graphic design for leading magazines in New York, and finally began his own business in the less frantic world of northeast Pennsylvania. In his adult social and professional life in publishing he had never assumed that he would not be accepted, but church was a different matter. He did not accompany Charles to church in nearby New Jersey. He respected and supported Charles as a Christian and a member of the clergy, but kept his distance. Nonetheless, something remained unresolved for him. This began to change as it occurred to him that if he had anger toward the church and its position, that was for him to deal with: he had to get on with his life spiritually as well as professionally and socially. So one Sunday morning when he was in his forties, at twenty after nine, he decided to go to church after dreaming the night before of his mother saying, "Bobby, go to church." The nearest church was Christ Church in Stroudsburg, Pennsylvania, and there he went, and there he stayed. The relationship has grown, and Bob has become active in diocesan life; with Charles he hosts a summer event for the Integrity chapter.

Today Bob is senior warden of Christ Church, but that did not come all at once. At first he was not very revealing of who he was sexually, as that was not why he was in church, but eventually, he says, "my worst fears" were realized and he was outed by circumstances not of his making. The conflict began when a priest was called to be rector, and when his gay sexuality became known, the call was revoked and considerable conflict arose in the parish, some of argument being quite harsh and personally aimed. The woman who finally did come as rector chose Bob as her senior warden, to the shock and intense anger of some. The conflict was a moment of transformation for Bob, however.

Bob found that because he was gay he "was evicted" from his parish — but "I refused to go." He adds that he learned that "I had more control of the situation than I thought I did." He could control his own response to the situation and realized that something was at stake in how he responded. When he was in the most agony over his parish membership a trusted friend told him, "They need you to stay." That is what he did, although some parishioners who were opposed to the presence of gay people in the parish did leave for the nearby Methodist congregation. He found that his most important testimony was simply a ministry of "being myself in the pew," although for a while he was alone in that pew. Soon one or two others from the straight majority of the parish would quietly join him in his pew, and the community began to change.

Bob reports that his growth was accomplished in his learning that "I have the capacity to forgive. . . . This is absolutely necessary for survival." His nonhostile presence made reconciliation possible with his fiercest attacker, and today Bob is the lay leader of the parish, even though for many years he found public meetings a daunting experience. Charles observes that Bob, a devout introvert, has become a very good public speaker and leader.

Bob reports that he had been willing to undergo the pain of remaining in his pew in part out of sense of mission to the church. It was not an easy decision, but he had been warned that "if you

leave now, they won't change for twenty-five years." His commitment to that change and his hope for that change kept him in
his pew, sometimes despite experiences of alienation. Charles, not
a frequent worshiper at Christ Church, observes that change did
occur and is now palpable: "the place is more open, happy." He
adds that "people are actually social at social times," in distinc-
tion to the time when Bob was confirmed and nobody talked to
visitors.

Bob is clear about the change in the parish. "It is no longer
a safe haven for people who are afraid that their world is gone,"
but a place that embraces a call to be the harbinger of a different
world.

Charles and Bob met at a friend's house In New York on what
happened to be Gay Pride weekend, on June 27, 1975. It was
love at first sight, and, Bob reports, "I just shut the book." The
following day they marched together in the parade. The next week
Charles invited Bob for dinner at his home in New Jersey "and he
just never left." For the next fifteen years Bob walked down the hill
each morning to get the train to New York, and Charles walked
up the hill to his university.

Neither Charles nor Bob is interested in marriage, a word with
which they simply do not identify. At the same time, they are grateful for moments of ritual support from the Christian community,
and Bob reports that "Bishop Spong practically married us" at
Charles's ordination. After Charles was vested as a priest in the
ordination liturgy, the bishop observed to the five hundred people
present, "We are here to bless Charles...but we all know that
Charles would not be the priest he is if it weren't for Bob, so we
are here to bless them both." The church was completely silent for
a moment, then prolonged applause began.

Reflecting on that moment, Bob remarked that it was un-
planned, unexpected, and quite meaningful. It was also a lesson
in leadership for him, because it demonstrated what can happen
when "the moral leader of a community takes the mike to say
things like that. We couldn't have done that on our own." He

cites a similar moment of recognition by a trustee of Charles's university at his retirement. When Charles thanked the president of Drew University for providing health benefits for domestic partners, he got a response he still cherishes. President Thomas Kean said, "Thank you for your appreciation, Charles, but this should have happened a long time ago; this is just a matter of justice." Reflecting on these times, Bob sees that there were several moments when, figuratively at least, "our heterosexual friends took us to the altar." Charles adds that "it was the community saying yes...so many people of good will — they want to bless."

Nonetheless, Bob and Charles are not drawn to the language of marriage or spousal relations. Their vocabulary has moved over the decades, though, and where they once simply referred to each other as friend, they now say partner. They do not wear rings, but neither one wears any jewelry, citing their devotion to gardening. "I would welcome wearing a ring if I wore rings," one of them added.

On the question of blessing liturgies, they are quite clear: "We wouldn't see ourselves that way." Charles adds that they have an understated quality to their relationship and do not engage in public displays of affection. He says that he and Bob know few of their contemporaries who want such rites and perceive those who do as having political as well as religious aims. He says that they already feel blessed by the church. After a little more conversation he returned to this question, and speaking of a liturgy in Christ Church, added, "I could well imagine that if I were more a part of that community, I would want that."

Charles believes that the church is still looking for language. From his point of view, same-sex unions and the marriage of a man and a woman are very different things, and if there are to be liturgies, "they must recognize gay people for what they are and what they have achieved despite some hardship," and employ a distinct vocabulary. He believes that he and Bob have "a holy union," but would not be willing to call it a marriage.

Although Charles and Bob feel no urgency about further liturgical affirmation, they do hope that they will be able to enter a civil union with the legal rights that it would bring.

It may be possible that their minds will change on this topic, and I have not asked them about that. However, in response to a draft of this chapter I sent them to check accuracy, Bob wrote to say that he and Charles had just returned from the wedding of two of their friends, both women, at Harvard's Memorial Church. The liturgy was celebrated on Independence Day, with Bishop Stephen Charleston presiding and Peter Gomes preaching. Bob reported that the outpouring of community support was intense as friends, colleagues, and students came out to pray with the couple. Bob concluded, "The wedding ended with the singing of 'My country, 'tis of thee, sweet land of liberty.' That put marriage in its true context."

Part Two

RITES

Chapter Three

General Observations

S ome of the people whom I have heard speak in support of liturgies blessing same-sex unions have never
witnessed a blessing service or examined the text of such
a rite. More, if not all, of the people I have heard speak against
these liturgies have never seen a rite celebrated or read a liturgical
text blessing a same-sex couple.

This situation is perhaps understandable given the limited
availability of the texts, but it is not useful if discussion of the issue
is to be informed by something other than aspiration or apprehen-
sion. It is to give some context for discussion of the *liturgical* and
pastoral questions about same-sex rites that this section has been
written. Those who come to this book looking for a theoretical debate will go away empty.[1] The goal here is to give a general picture
of what is being done among those now shaping rites. By looking
at the rites merely as rites, some readers who find the very question
of same-sex unions upsetting may find themselves desensitized to
the extent that the topic can be discussed with relative equanimity.
There is, then, a sense in which I hope this section is boring, as it
treats this liturgical data like any other liturgical data. That means
above all that it tries to ask how these liturgies are constructed and
how they work. There is another sense in which it is hoped that

---

1. The reader who wishes highly readable introductions to the biblical and theological
questions setting forth reasons to bless unions is directed to Gray Temple, *Gay Unions*
(New York: Church Publishing, 2004), where something of a dialogue between progressive
and conservative thought takes place. Temple helps the reader distinguish between the
canonical text and quasi-canonical interpretation of texts. J. Neil Alexander, *This Far by
Grace* (Cambridge, Mass.: Cowley, 2003), is a moving report of an intellectual, emotional,
and spiritual journey through the questions of sexuality. Walter Wink, *Homosexuality and
Christian Faith* (Minneapolis: Fortress, 1999) is a standard work on the subject.

the material is boring: these liturgies are the work of traditional Episcopalians, and all reflect a great care about liturgical language and the cohesion of liturgical units. I have never encountered one that indulges in the use of an outrageous word or act, or anything designed to shock. All are liturgically modest and generally reflect mainstream Anglican liturgical piety.

While I do hope that scholarship has sharpened my eye sufficiently to enable me to make useful comments on the structure and flow of the rites, it should be noted from the first that the analysis that follows, like the rest of the book, is planned as an introduction for the general reader. It does not attempt to make an in-depth study for scholars, even less for the debaters of this age. Writing without recourse to a host of footnotes is a form of working without a net and has provided a few chills for this writer when the urge to qualify, self-protect, or expatiate had to be suppressed.

That said, in identifying our subject matter liturgically we must begin with one key question that Anne and Brenda raise: Are we discussing marriage rites here? Some insist that the name of "marriage" not be invoked because of the absence of civil status for the union in most jurisdictions; others insist as strongly that same-sex unions are sacramentally the same thing as marriage. Others, like Bob and Charles, believe the two acts are essentially different. Regardless of the civil debate, in the vocabulary of church debate at present, the marriage-like nature of the rites and the relationships celebrated in them is often downplayed in an understandable effort to avoid the distraction that debate about a single word would surely bring. Additionally, some bishops who tolerate rites have made it clear that they should in no way resemble a marriage. We must face that question here, however, to know what we are looking at.

The liturgies examined reflect the unsettled nature of this question in that they bring many names to what they celebrate. A few are flatly called "marriage," and we have seen that Brenda and Anne refer to their "wedding." More typically, "union" (in English, just a synonym for marriage!) and "covenant" are used.

Perhaps the most unusual title I have seen is "A Celebration of the Enhancement of the Lives of *N.* and *N.*" Whether they designate marriage or enhanced life, it is nonetheless true that the various names refer to one class of ritual act: the recognition and celebration of what might neutrally be called a household, domestic unit, bonded pair, or family, where the interpersonal bond includes the giving of the two persons to each other physically. The common factor is the public observance of the joining of two people who will share their lives with each other in body and spirit.

When trying to make a point about what a ritual actually is, teachers of liturgy habitually refer to "the anthropologist from Mars," an investigator who knows nothing of our languages and simply watches what happens and classifies the big picture. Thus, the anthropologist from Mars who sees couples of whatever composition enter an assembly of friends in a sacred or special space, make promises, join hands, exchange tokens of commitment, and then embrace would say that all of them are specimens of an earth-person ritual about a joining of two people usually called marriage, regardless of the sex of those being united. To put it nontechnically, it looks like a duck.

This is not to quibble about a name, but to ask a sacramental, liturgical, and pastoral question. In addition to the fact that they look like, sound like, and ritually flow like marriage rites, the liturgies examined here have been semiofficially determined to be such. In response to a General Convention resolution, a survey of scholarship was authorized in 1996 by the Standing Liturgical Commission and the Theology Committee of the House of Bishops of the Episcopal Church. Among its conclusions is the observation that no matter what the rites are called, where a covenanted commitment is made in love, intended for life, and expressed in part through sexual intercourse, what amounts to sacramental marriage is intended. Sacramental marriage is understood to bear grace to the couple and through them to the human community. Simply in terms of what to call what the church is doing, civil consequences are immaterial, but the matter is never that simple in practice, so the use or avoidance of the vocabulary of marriage will surely remain an unsettled question for the foreseeable future. It is of interest that in Canada, the first rite used in the Diocese of New Westminster was entitled "The Blessing of Same-Sex Unions" while the May 2003 version is entitled "The Celebration of a Covenant" (see Liturgies Three and Four below, pp. 115 and 123).

In liturgical vocabulary, the answer is more nearly clear. Surveying most of the ritual material indicates that for gay and lesbian Episcopalians, the preferred ritual is one very like an opposite-sex marriage. As one studies the texts arising in this country, one is struck by how often they are based directly on the Prayer Book marriage rite. In these cases, besides the necessary adjustments in gendered language, the only consistent difference in character between same-sex marriages and opposite-sex marriages is general lack of reference to the generative function of marriage: male-female couples usually can produce children and very often do, and the marriage rite reflects this. However, mere biology does not settle the question. Although the idea has not been widely expressed liturgically, many gay and lesbian writers point out that there is more than one way for a marriage (same- or opposite-sex) to be generative: the care and nurture of those already in the world may be a mission more excellently fulfilled by those who do not have the concerns of child-rearing. Of course, some same-sex couples, male or female, do adopt and raise children, and some lesbian women bear children conceived with donor sperm. From this point of view, it is sometimes also argued that all couples of any kind have a number of generative functions other than child-bearing and child-rearing. Certainly those of us heterosexuals now beyond the child-bearing and child-rearing years would hope not to be as good as dead as far as our contribution to the life of the community is concerned, but this idea seems not yet to have been cast in liturgical language for opposite-sex couples marrying late in life.

The question of generative contribution to society has been addressed by David Nimmons in *The Soul Beneath the Skin*.[2] Looking at gay men, Nimmons finds them contributing to society in unique ways. His study shows much higher rates of altruism, a reinvention of male community, and a workable approach to the question of how men can maintain real friendships with women. Malcolm Boyd has affirmed that lesbian and gay people have a distinct vocation in the world and even speaks of this commitment as "a kind of perpetual Peace Corps. We are meant," he adds, "for something beyond our own concerns."

Again, it should come as no surprise that most of the liturgies produced by Episcopalians are either direct adaptations of the marriage rite of the 1979 Book of Common Prayer, or else follow its pattern or "shape," with some excisions and supplements. That pattern to be observed in the Prayer Book is what is called a "ritual mass" in liturgical studies. That is, marriage, like baptism, confirmation, ordination, and so on, occurs within a celebration of the Eucharist, almost always concluding its special task before the exchange of the Peace. The liturgical shape observed in the Prayer Book marriage rite is a simple one:

Entrance
Address to the Assembly
Declaration of Consent
Collect and Liturgy of the Word (through the Sermon [and Creed])
Exchange of Vows
Exchange of Rings (and/or Other Symbols)
Pronouncement of the Marriage (concluding "let no one put asunder")
Prayers of the People
Blessing the Marriage ("nuptial blessing")
The Peace

2. David Nimmons, *The Soul Beneath the Skin: The Unseen Hearts and Habits of Gay Men* (New York: St. Martin's Press, 2002).

The Eucharist continues from the Offertory.

The rites examined here all follow this pattern, although one unit may be occasionally missing, or several units compressed into one.

Generally the authors of the same-sex rites that concern us here intend to express the liturgical equivalency of same-sex with opposite-sex marriages. They do so in terms of both the sacramental character of the rite and the moral/relational equivalency of the union contracted in the rite. Therefore the same-sex rites often also attempt to assure the participants that their relationship is just as sacred — and as blessed — as those of opposite-sex couples, and this is usually done in an opening address at the "Dearly Beloved" place in the beginning of the rite. The note of teaching that normally sounds in the opening address often takes a prophetic tone as well. The key biblical motif in these liturgies is covenant-making, rather than recollection of Eden or the wedding at Cana. Because the 1979 marriage rite also uses the language of covenant, the idea has been identified as a common foundation on which to build a single rite for couples of all kinds.

Not everyone agrees that the liturgical pattern these rites should follow is that of marriage, but those Christians who avoid the marriage model are writing from outside the Episcopal Church more often than from within. Some rites that are beyond our scope here are the work of those who believe in the sacredness of their commitments but who find the whole pattern of "marriage" as it is known in most of the world oppressive, and thus do not wish to imply marriage in the ordinary sense. The fact that there is no unanimity among gay and lesbian people about the relationship of their unions to conventional marriage is hardly surprising in a culture where very many opposite-sex couples have avoided marriage, and sometimes have done so because they also share doubts about the value of the social institution called marriage. Same- or opposite-sex, some couples wish to avoid the restrictions and impoverishment that they perceive Eastern or Western marriage to have placed on individuals, particularly on women.

It is not possible to study the content of absent rites, but it is nonetheless important to point out that for many same-sex couples of any religious denomination there remains little or no interest in celebrating or blessing their unions in the church. Both partners may in fact be practicing Christians, but the historical attitude of Christianity to homosexuality, or the perception that their union finds no easy equivalent in the church's bag of liturgical resources, or both, has resulted in a lack of interest in (or determination to avoid) religious ceremony. A search of the Internet will reveal scores of businesses or services geared toward assisting same-sex couples in crafting an event to celebrate their union in contexts other than the liturgy.

Within the Episcopal Church, in some dioceses the bishop has encouraged the use of the Blessing of a Home in the *Book of Occasional Services* as an alternative to a marriage-like service. In some cases, this is considered a doing of all that is possible in the absence of approved rites. In others, the house blessing has value for those who desire ritual recognition of their shared life but balk at the idea of marriage.

Although it can be pointed out that diocesan bishops may set forth liturgical material for occasions not provided for in the Book of Common Prayer, only a handful have done so for the unions that concern us here. Although it could be argued that what is not forbidden is permitted, the fact that enabling legislation on the national level has failed passage has signaled otherwise to some bishops. The noninhibitory language of 2003 has signaled to some bishops and communities a greater freedom to produce rites, and at the moment of this writing, Washington, D.C., and Vermont have produced diocesan liturgies (see pp. 135 and 144 below).

The question of the right of a bishop to issue liturgies (the so-called *ius liturgicum*) has been addressed at the Lambeth Conference since 1867. In 1897 the bishops wrote that they thought it their "duty to affirm the right of every Bishop, within the jurisdiction assigned to him by the church, to set forth or to sanction additional services and prayers when he believes that God's work may be thereby furthered, or the spiritual needs of the worshippers more fully met." At the same time they insisted that "this power must always be subject to any limitations imposed by the provincial or other lawful authority, and the utmost care must be taken that all such additions or adaptations be in thorough harmony with the spirit and tenor of the whole Book." Given that the Episcopal Church has recognized that those dioceses or communities experimented with same-sex blessings are operating within bounds, it seems that in this province the requirements of the Lambeth bishops are being met. Nonetheless, it is impossible to imagine that the writers just quoted contemplated the implications of their words for our present question.

How the principles of revision and the *ius liturgicum* have been studied and adopted by the Diocese of New Westminster may be seen at their website (www.vancouver.anglican.ca), where the reader will find a learned and stimulating essay by Richard Leggett of the Vancouver School of Theology. The reader who finds the entire topic of same-sex unions of interest in the ecumenical or interfaith context cannot do better than to start with the resources provided by the Unitarian-Universalist Association, readily accessible on the Internet (www.uua.org). Jewish resources come almost entirely from the Reconstructionist strand of the Jewish tradition. Internet addresses change rapidly, so the interested reader is encouraged simply to search under the words "same-sex" and "union," or similar pairs.

Precedent

Some eight years ago I expressed, in what I thought was a local document relating to a specific event, the opinion that there is no precedent for same-sex rites in the Anglican liturgical tradition, in my view a statement remarkable only for its obviousness. It seems clear that if the Episcopal Church is to set forth rites for blessing same-sex unions it will be with the understanding that it is not Anglican precedent but new perceptions of God's will that guide the action. If so, it would not be the first time God's people had heard the words, "Behold, I do a new thing." In 1996 my observation caused hurt in some places and outrage in others, but as is too often the case, there was no dialogue nor were questions about the observation addressed to me.

Those outraged most often made their appeal to John Boswell's *Same-Sex Unions in Premodern Europe.*[3] Those appealing to that work tend not to note that the late professor of history was not interested in the Anglican tradition, but looked at much earlier material in a different part of the world. Beyond that, it needs to be said that the overwhelming majority of historical and liturgical scholars who have reviewed Boswell's work (even those who may share passionately his desire to see same-sex blessings in the church) are not convinced by his argument, and some take significant exception to it. Liturgical scholars among them point out that the "secret" or "unknown" rites he "discovered" were neither secret nor unknown, and most are discussed by Byzantine specialists as being exactly what they appear to be: rites recognizing deep and abiding friendship. Because Boswell believed the texts to be unknown, he did not consult with liturgical scholars and came to what most liturgists consider to be an unsupportable view of those texts. This lack of consultation led to unhelpful conclusions when looking at texts celebrating friendships between men who had taken vows that prohibited them from enjoying sexual congress of any kind. One of the rites he takes to be one of sexual union is in fact entitled in Greek "the making of brothers," and the very brief prose nowhere even hints at physical union. In 2003 Harvard University Press published Louis Crompton's encyclopedic *Homosexuality and Civilization.* Crompton corrects point-by-point the thesis that there ever was a golden age of urban Christian celebration of homosexuality.

While it may be said that Boswell's project regarding male relationships has failed, the case is not so clear with women at this

---

3. John Boswell, *Same-Sex Unions in Premodern Europe* (New York: Villard Books, 1994).

writing. Research is not conclusive, but there are indications of quasi-underground rites for women in the Middle Ages.

All of that said, the study of the rites for the "making of brothers" does raise an important point. We can by no means dismiss Boswell's project in the larger sense in which it represents everyone's search for solidarity and continuity with a past. It is what human beings do in understanding and affirming their identities. Whatever their limitations, Boswell's researches do put us in contact with a lost tradition of ritually recognizing deep friendships. Because the very real homophobia of our American culture makes it difficult even to mention, let alone describe, passionate friendship between men (except in the context of war and its grisly subset, team athletics), Boswell's texts do startle us into remembering that for the most part we do not have what David and Jonathan had — the possibility of making a covenant, of formally committing to the discipline of friendship.[4] In the collection of texts in part 3 of this study I have included a union rite based on Boswell's research (see below p. 131).

The search for solidarity is also the search for solidarity with couples joined in traditional marriage. It can be argued that the marriage template fits the liturgies we will examine because they reach out for solidarity with all couples everywhere. In sum, while Boswell's liturgical conclusions are not in my view supportable, it seems unwise to dismiss the underlying search of same-sex couples for connection with a tradition and for solidarity with the contemporary community of committed couples.

There is a larger problem with an appeal to Boswell's or anyone else's antiquarian excavations, however. It seems fundamentally wrong to believe that a theological and liturgical problem of this size can be solved by appealing primarily to liturgical

---

4. Temple argues that David had conquered Jonathan romantically and sexually, at least in the eyes of Saul. Saul's objections in 1 Samuel 20:30–33 certainly do sound sexual, but the seal on such a relationship would not have been a covenant alone, but the union of their bodies. Regardless of what one makes of the theory that David and Jonathan were lovers, the covenant between them was certainly of an order surpassing that of a casual sexual liaison, which seems to be the point of the biblical passages in any case.

precedent (or its absence). This tendency to seek precedent has already cursed Christianity with patristic or other equally quaint fundamentalisms in many areas of liturgical life. The fact is that "precedent" can be found in liturgical history for any number of things that would amuse, astound, or outrage the reader. Leaving the question of marriage aside, it remains true that within the Anglican Communion clergy with too much time on their hands have searched out or stumbled upon precedent for the most exotic liturgical stunts or habiliments. This has the sad effect of making Anglicans something of a joke to the more settled liturgical churches, and gives serious liturgical inquiry a black eye. The problem before us needs to be settled on its own liturgical, theological, and pastoral merits rather than by archaeology.

Along with my belief that if anything were to be done, we are in new rather than forgotten territory, the other bias to which I should confess is my belief that it is somewhere between naiveté and fatuousness to suggest that liturgical texts are just somehow *there* and that we simply deduce our theology from them (the modern myth of *lex orandi*). The reality is that from our faith and experience we shape liturgies that in turn reshape us as we encounter the world, prompting us to reshape the rites, and on and on. The relationship of liturgy and faith is reciprocal.[5] Looking carefully at a rite may indeed tell us something of the faith of those who shaped it, but that settles nothing about what the rite will mean in today's context, and how our experience of it and our world may direct its revision or replacement tomorrow. Any liturgy that is not a work in progress may well have ceased to be liturgy and become an idol or an irrelevance, perhaps both.

The rites to which we will attend here are very much works in progress: the liturgy of the "Second Consultation," for example, on the blessing of same-sex unions is understood by its authors as a

5. Gordon Lathrop, *Holy Things: A Liturgical Theology* (Minneapolis: Fortress, 1993), is a very readable presentation of the other point of view, that rite conditions us, period. He finds the law-gospel tension inherent in the "juxtaposition" of elements in liturgy, although from a non-Lutheran point of view this position may not be very compelling.

model not ready for celebration. Thus nothing studied here can in any way be perceived as anyone's final judgment of what "ought" to be the form and manner of celebrating unions, something that is to be determined by the church. The fact that the Diocese of New Westminster has produced two very different rites in two years is stunning evidence of the fluidity of the situation in which we find ourselves. In what follows, connection or comparison is made with the Prayer Book marriage service to illustrate how the liturgical development of same-sex rites is an organic process to be understood within the context of the church's overall liturgical development, not to urge that connection as a pattern that ought to be followed or that is itself incapable of reform.

Regardless of the path the church follows with regard to same-sex unions, I believe that some of the materials created in the pursuit of liturgies for those unions provide material to be considered when marriage rites of any kind are next revised.

The unofficial archives of the liturgical officer of the Episcopal Church contain many more services than could possibly be listed here, and I draw from a few that seem to be the most representative or seminal. We will direct our brief study to three rites in particular. The first is Anne and Brenda Bost's liturgy celebrated in late 2002 in New York City, a practical example placed beside the two more general rites (see Liturgy One, p. 99 below). The second is included in the "Second Report" of the Consultation on Same-Sex Unions, a group of scholars and others who issued two substantial reports in the 1990s (see Liturgy Two, p. 105 below). The third is that of the Diocese of New Westminster, the Canadian diocese that has attracted attention for its official endorsement of same-sex blessings, in original and revised versions (see Liturgies Three and Four, pp. 115 and 123 below).

Frequent reference will also be made to material from a number of parishes where there is experience with these liturgies for some years, and from a model rite produced in the Diocese of California.

Chapter Four

Witness and Bless

E very society, religious or otherwise, regulates pair bonding and reproduction. Marriage is a civil institution before it is a religious institution. How did the Christian church get into the "marriage business"? Marriage as we know it is the one principal Christian liturgical act without precedent in Jewish prayer. This is in part because what we would identify as Jewish marriage liturgies postdate the origins of Christianity. This is not to say that Jews did not marry, of course, but to underscore that neither temple nor synagogue, priests nor rabbis, are known to have played a role in Jewish marriages as Christianity arose. What first-century Jews did have was a procession from the bride's house to her new home, where the party began. The exchange of property and other arrangements had taken place separately in both time and place.[1]

It is from pre-Christian Roman life that familiar marriage customs come: the ring, the witnesses, the threshold, the veil, and so on. The Roman act also involved the taking of auspices, sacrifice, and the party, the festivities ending with tucking the couple into bed for their first night as a married couple. It was not unknown for the consummation of the marriage to be witnessed as well.[2] The one anthropological constant that comprehends Jewish and

---

1. Absolutely essential reading for this section on the "marriage business" is Kenneth Stevenson, *Nuptial Blessing* (New York: Oxford University Press, 1985). See also Edward Muir, *Ritual in Early Modern Europe* (Cambridge: Cambridge University Press, 1997), and Christopher Brooke, *The Medieval Idea of Marriage* (Oxford: Oxford University Press, 1989).
2. Paul Veyne's *A History of Private Life: From Pagan Rome to Byzantium* (Cambridge, Mass.: Belknap, 1992), relates details of Roman marriage, which came in several forms; some of those details are not for the squeamish.

Greco-Roman weddings is the realization that when people begin life as a couple, there will be a party.

Christians, who were quickly to become a non-Jewish community, adapted the Roman practice to their own beliefs, but this did not immediately result in services of worship. The bishop, as leader of the community, was sometimes asked to approve of an engagement. Then came a period where a blessing was imparted (sometimes even at the traditional tucking-in), but only slowly did the creation of liturgies for marriage begin. As the imperial culture morphed into Christendom, the increasingly liturgical event blended with the civil act with legal consequences. At first, the bishop or a presbyter may simply have taken over the role of the *auspex nuptiarum,* who presided at the joining of the couple, and as the *pronuba,* who blessed the marriage bed. Just as the Eucharist came to replace the Roman meal at the grave, so it came in time to replace the nuptial sacrifices — at this point the bishop or presbyter would have had an essential role. The church ultimately became the custodian of this civil (not secular!) aspect of life, and although in the century before the Reformation the majority of marriages in the dioceses of Ely (73 percent) and Canterbury (92 percent), for instance, had no religious ceremony, they were still recorded in the parish register as marriages. Muir reports that in Wales marriage was accomplished by the couple publicly jumping over a broom — and divorce by jumping back.

It would only be with the Council of Trent that Roman Catholics would be required to be married by a priest, and in a church building. There had been movement toward this moment. The trend to church weddings had certainly grown in the upper strata of society, especially since the Fourth Lateran Council of 1215 had listed marriage as a sacrament, but it is to be noted that the medieval theologians did not regard this sacrament as anything the church administered. The "form" (required words) of the sacrament was the exchange of vows, and the "matter" (things and acts) was the physical consummation of the marriage. Despite this official theology, more and more emphasis began to be placed on

the priestly blessing of the marriage, as an aid to fidelity and fecundity, as a protection from evil, and to control secret marriages
(those undertaken without parental consent).

The Reformation insistence that marriage was just as sacred
a vocation as the totally abstinent life in convent or monastery
had liturgical impact. Eventually the civil contract (often carried
out on the church steps) became the giving of consent (with the
now-optional "giving away"), and was taken inside the church
building and into the liturgical rite for members of the Church of
England and the Roman Catholic Church. In Cranmer's scheme,
the declaration of consent was the assurance given of the parties'
free intention to enter the relationship about to be blessed, even
though marriages were sometimes arranged or even contracted
without more than acquiescence on the part of those being married. It boiled down for some to the declaration that one knew
what he or she was doing, even though by our standards the choice
was not free. It is intriguing that some of those who most strongly
advocate the church's getting out of the "business" of marriage
generally retain liturgically the most nearly secular of the components of the marriage rite, the consent and the "giving away" or
"presentation."

Edwin Friedman sometimes told the story of a rabbi who was
flown in a private plane at some expense to a resort where he was
to conduct a wedding. He was met at the plane by the couple,
who almost immediately explained that due to scheduling pres-
sures from the catering hall, the actual ceremony would have to
be as brief as possible. He stared at them for a second and said,
"Do you want to be married?" They replied, "Why, yes." The
rabbi replied, "You are," and got back into the plane. While the
"minimum form" recognized by Christian writers is a little more
complex than this, his point applies to the Christian situation.

Similarly, on the legal side, most people do not realize that a
"marriage license" does not give a couple permission to get married. The license is addressed to the cleric or other officiant, gives
him or her permission to function for the state by presiding at and

recording the civil marriage, and requires that within a certain time period the officiant is to report the marriage. From a legal point of view, none of the material represented in the church vows or blessing is necessary; what is necessary is the statement that one lawfully enters into a marriage with the other.

As we will see, necessity has become something of a virtue, as from Cranmer's time on declarations of consent have been embroidered upon, taking up more liturgical air time and carrying more theological freight than their original function requires. This is true in the union of both same- and opposite-sex couples. If the church is to get out of the business end of marriage, the language of the civil pact will require transformation or elimination.

It could also be argued, under Bishop Rowthorn's poetic observation, "Lord, you make the common holy," that the civil portion of the rite can be seen by the Christian to be the language of covenant, an initial or introductory celebration of the couple's intention to exchange the most solemn of vows. Some commentators identify this as a kind of "betrothal" ceremony within the marriage rite, and the Consultation provides for a moment of publicly stating intent long before the union takes place.

In the Prayer Book service, after the opening address the officiant asks, "will you," indicating that a covenant has still to be completed, as it will be when vows are finally recited:

> N., will you have this man/woman to be your husband/wife; to live together in the covenant of marriage? Will you love him/her, comfort him/her, honor and keep him/her, in sickness and in health; and, forsaking all others, be faithful to him/her as long as you both shall live?

In sum, this form asks if it is the person's will to enter marriage, to love the other regardless of circumstances, and to do so for life.

In the Bosts' service, there is no introductory declaration of consent or betrothal. Nor was there any presentation or giving away except for what was done tacitly in the two women being brought to the altar by a father and a son — the practice of males escorting females was a piece of tradition they did not choose to alter. At no point were Anne and Brenda asked about intent, although they were asked what they were seeking, namely, the blessing. The original New Westminster liturgy also waits for the time after the sermon, and does have a "what do you seek" question, but it is under a section entitled "Intent." After the couple asks for a blessing from God and the community, the one presiding asks each of them in words reminiscent of the marriage rite,

> N.N., will you share your love and life with N.N., your wholeness and your brokenness, your joys and your sorrows, your health and your sickness, your riches and your poverty, your success and your failure, and be faithful to *him/her* so long as you both shall live?

The newer Canadian version omits this Declaration of Intent entirely and compresses all promises into the act of covenanting. The position paper that accompanies the rite emphasizes that this covenant is to be understood as distinct from that in the marriage service.

The next section in the first New Westminster rite is called Support and Blessing of the Community. Here the assembly promises to support the couple; in the next question they are asked, "Do you give them your blessing?" After all of this the one presiding recounts that the couple has been prepared and has stated their intent; there follows the announcement that in a moment they will exchange vows and gifts. This pattern is repeated in the 2003 New Westminster rite, although explicit reference is no longer made to the exchange or rings or other gifts.

As already indicated, the 1996 Report of the Consultation prefers that the Declaration of Intent take place well before celebration of the rest of the rite, as the beginning of "a time of exploration," something like an engagement. If this is not done, the briefest possible declaration is used in the final rite, but none of the actual service folders I have seen reflect the desired use, with some placing the fuller form of intent in a place parallel to the consent in the Prayer Book marriage rite. The couple have the first words in this section, announcing their desire to share their joy and be given the "support and prayers" of the assembly. They are each asked, by Christian name only, "do you freely intend to commit yourself to N as your partner in life?" The simple response, "I do" is followed by a theme that will appear throughout the rite, likely to be loved or hated by equal numbers of people, as each party says, "Blessed be God who appears to me in N.'s love." The sponsors will later say, "Blessed be God who appears to us in their love." As the intent section moves on, the people very soon repeat this antiphon, twice. It occurs again at the Vows, after the Exchange of Rings, and at the Blessing, for a total of eight repetitions. Whether or not this phrase and its ostinato employment amount to good liturgy (I think not), the union is clearly portrayed as having a purpose beyond the life of the couple. The Intent section of the Consultation liturgy concludes with the sponsors, and then the entire assembly, promising support of the couple in their life together.

Because they envision this marking of Intent as a separate event from the actual celebration and blessing, the designers of the Consultation rite provide for it to conclude with a substantial prayer and the optional laying-on of hands.

The rite adopted at St. Thomas Parish in Washington, D.C., provides a single marriage liturgy for couples of any composition, and thus its Declaration of Consent is very like that of the Prayer Book (love, comfort, honor, and keep, etc.), but with the addition of the hallmark of the same-sex rites, sponsors, whose support is asked before that of the assembly as a whole.

All Saints' Church in Pasadena, California, has been prepared to bless same-sex unions since 1990, and parishioners have produced many variations on its pattern for blessing unions. In all of the examples I have seen from that parish, the Declaration of Consent (rather than Intent) follows the opening address. Of the major sources of liturgical material, All Saints is notable in not making use of sponsors, and its liturgy in many ways resembles a rite created for its northern neighbors in the Diocese of California.

When the consent or intent is placed in the opening moments, as in the Prayer Book rite, the promise of the assembly to support the couple is always followed by a collect. There are also rites where a collect follows when the Declaration of Intent takes place after the sermon. Some of these use the familiar collect (page 425 in the Prayer Book), simply changing "this man and this woman" to the same sex. In the original New Westminster rite, where the Intent comes late in the service, it is separated from the vows by a collect that still uses both the Christian and surnames of each party. This prayer serves as the Collect of the Day in the Consultation liturgy, although surnames are not used:

> O God our Creator, lover of heaven and earth, you have taught us to love each other as Christ loved us, to bear each other's burdens, and to share each other's strengths. Look with favor upon *N.N.* and *N.N.*, whom you have brought together in love. Grant them sincere love and unfailing strength. Protect them in their life and in their work, and lead them with us and all creation into your realm of justice and peace. We ask this through...

Witness

Cranmer originally envisioned the marriage rite as taking place just before the parish Eucharist on a Sunday, a vision also held by the continental reformer Martin Bucer. Not only was marriage to be public, it was to be a celebration acknowledged by the entire parish community. This experiment was not to survive as rubric, but the practice is occasionally seen today among opposite-sex couples. The union liturgy of the Consultation prefers just this setting. Even where this preference is not followed, almost all unions take place in a large gathering of some sort, and that gathering is called to witness.

"Witness" has more than one meaning here, and those meanings occur simultaneously. Contracts require witnesses, providing testimony that the arrangement was entered into as described and proving that the parties really did enter into it themselves and did indeed sign the necessary papers. This function of witness can be fulfilled by anyone of legal age. Those same-sex rites inquired into here have much richer expectations. Witness is also testimony *about* the sacredness of the united condition of the couple. Witness is also testimony *to* the couple of the community's support of the couple and the esteem in which it holds the state into which they are entering. Finally, in virtually all of the rites, there is the expectation that the couple's ongoing relationship will bear testimony *to the community* and others to the transforming grace of God. The Consultation's antiphon blessing the God who is revealed in the couple's love puts this idea in sharpest focus, and we shall see it reflected in the prayers and opening address of rites from many sources, although no other liturgies put the burden of theophany on a couple's efforts to live together.

The address that begins the Consultation rite is the most compact:

> Welcome to the celebration of N. and N.'s commitment to each other as life partners. The Christian community recognizes that the love between two people manifests God's love. Today we celebrate N. and N.'s love as a gift from God to them and to all of us. As they formally commit to their life together, we bless and thank God for this gift to us.

This is both a compact recitation of what theologians call the "goods" of the relationship (love as a gift) and the insistence that it affects all people. In the 1549 Prayer Book, Cranmer listed three chief goods of marriage in this order:

> One cause was the procreacion of children, to be brought up in the feare and nurture of the Lord, and prayse of God. Secondly it was ordeined for a remedie agaynst sinne, and to avoide fornicacion, that suche persones as bee maried, might live chastlie in matrimonie, and kepe themselves undefiled membres of Christes bodye. Thirdelye for the mutuall societie, helpe, and coumfort,

that the one oughte to have of thother, both in prosperitie and adversitie.

Cranmer's formula of children, chastity, and community survived into the 1662 book. Rather than reform that grim formula, no American book (1785, 1789, 1892, 1928) included any list until 1979, where the purposes are considerably different than those listed by the twice-married archbishop:

> The union of husband and wife in heart, body, and mind is intended by God for their mutual joy; for the help and comfort given one another in prosperity and adversity; and, when it is God's will, for the procreation of children and their nurture in the knowledge and love of the Lord.

Joy is listed first, community second, children third; chastity is not on the screen as a *purpose* of marriage, although it is mentioned as an *obligation* in a later section of the liturgy. This last point may reflect the fact that the 1979 Prayer Book was drafted in a time of sexual optimism, and that the Proposed Book (1976) that became the text of 1979 was adopted several years before HIV was identified. The idea that faithfulness might in fact be good for one spiritually, psychologically, and physically has had a slow rebirth, and it is noteworthy that the majority of the same-sex rites studied here in one way or another include the express commitment to forsake all others and be faithful to the partner. The Consultation rite addresses faithfulness in the giving of the ring. A number of liturgies, like the California rite, directly require that no other relationship, physical or otherwise, be put in competition with the union being celebrated, perhaps broadening the scope of faithfulness in a way deserving of consideration in the blessing of any union. A rite celebrated at St. George's Church in Glenn Dale, Maryland, does not use the language of covenant and fidelity, but prefers commitment and the Hebrew concept of *hesed*, steadfast or "covenant" love, an attribute of God's own self in the scriptures of Israel.

The goods of the relationship are defined carefully in the first New Westminster rite, which was itself modeled on the Prayer Book tradition, although the generative aspect of the relationship is not addressed. Interestingly, the first New Westminster rite speaks of the covenant between the two persons as having already been made:

> Beloved People of God, we have come together in the presence of God to witness and bless the covenant of love and fidelity which *N.N.* and *N.N.* have made with each other. The union of two persons in heart, body, and mind is intended by God for their mutual joy; for the help and comfort given one another in prosperity and adversity; and that their love may be a blessing to all whom they encounter. This solemn covenant is not to be entered into unadvisedly or lightly, but reverently, deliberately, and with the commitment to seek God's will for their lives.

This text has seen wide circulation, and had previously been used for some years at All Saints in Pasadena, although on one occasion at that church, there was included among the goods of this relationship the familiar "and, when it is God's will, for the procreation of children and their nurture in the knowledge and love of the Lord."

The second New Westminster rite backs away from this language entirely. The cleric presiding simply says:

> A covenant is an ancient form of promise, a public declaration of commitment that binds people in an enduring relationship. The Bible tells the story of God's covenant with human beings. God's covenant with Israel was the basis of the people's liberation from slavery and exile. God's covenant with the followers of Jesus brings us into a new community where there is no male or female, Jew nor Greek, slave nor free, but one people united in Christ. All our covenants with family and friends are signs of God's faithfulness and love. They are living expressions of God's promises to us and sources of hope to others.

The 2004 diocesan rite from Washington, D.C., does not have an opening address. Rather, it states the goods of the relationship in its opening Collect, which one notes is a single sentence:

> Holy and loving God, in our baptism you call us into relationship with you and the whole creation: We thank you for giving us signs of your steadfast love in the covenant of fidelity two people make with one another, and we pray that, in your mercy, you will give your blessing to N. and N., who come before you, and strengthen them day by day with the love of your Holy Spirit that they may be a blessing to one another and to the world; through Jesus Christ our Savior, who lives and reigns with you and the Holy Spirit, one God, for ever and ever. *Amen.*

In all the examples the witness to the community and the world is to the love of God reflected in the love of the couple, for their sake and for that of the community. Some texts include the observation that the laws of state and church do not recognize the bond being blessed. That of St. George's in Glenn Dale joins other same-sex rites that tackle the familiar New Testament–based recitation that traditional marriage "signifies to us the unity between Christ and the Church." Their rendition for same-sex couples is, "The bond between two people shows us the mystery of the union between God and God's people, and the Scriptures point to the centrality of steadfast Love as the principal sign of God's presence." A service leaflet without attribution attacks this seeming barrier very directly:

> We have come together in the presence of God, sharing the belief that the joining of two human beings, in heart, body, and mind, is a sign and sacrament of the intimate, loving relationship God desires with the community and has with the Church in Jesus Christ.

The single service to be used for opposite- and same-sex couples at St. Thomas in Washington takes familiar patterns and vocabulary to produce something that includes the Christ and

Church mystery but also invokes the history of the ancestors and the idea of household:

> We have come together to witness. . . . A bond and covenant of marriage/holy union was established by God in creation. God made our first parents for each other, and when they had fallen into sin, God created a new household by grace in Abraham and Sarah, through which all people might be blessed. In the fullness of time, Our Lord Jesus Christ, fruit of that household, gathered the Apostles together with himself to create a new family of God. Behold now the mystery of the union between N. and N., called by God to embody in their covenant that union between Christ and His Church.

In addition to holding up the expression "holy union" as a synonym for marriage (p. 424), the 1979 Prayer Book introduced Episcopalians to "covenant" as descriptive of the married relationship. The vast majority of same-sex rites adopt the language of covenant, and many writers have suggested it as the basis for a common rite to be used by same- and opposite-sex couples. The most common expression is "covenant of love and fidelity." The Consultation's liturgy consistently uses "commitment" rather than "covenant." It is also well to note that frequently the Prayer Book language of "holy union" has been adopted in blessings of same-sex rites.

Bless

When the history of late-twentieth-century Christianity is written and the topic of liturgical reform comes up, writers may well conclude that the second half of that century was a time of generalizations that were both inaccurate and damaging. Without stopping for lengthy analysis of the most infuriating mistake, that *leitourgia* means the work of the people (it means what is done for public good, and the implications are profound), we must spend a little time with what it means to bless.

The late tendency to reduce complex truths to bumper stick-ers or slogans is evident in the attempt, still alive in some places, to reduce the idea of blessing someone or something to that of giving thanks. This is an idea particularly popular among those who are nervous about blessing things, as though the inanimate or super-personal were not a part of creation or not still of use to God or God's people. The nervousness that blessing a thing or an abstraction such as a relationship might be an attempt at magic has driven another nail into the already well-sealed coffin of Western imagination. There are those, the architect of the latest New Westminster rite among them, who take a somewhat mod-erated view, and in addition to giving thanks are willing to see blessing as a naming of the qualities already inherent in persons or relationships.

In thinking through the question of blessing, we cannot stop here to ask the larger questions posed by linguistic philosophers, important as the questions are, but must limit our inquiry into "blessing" to the biblical and liturgical vocabulary of worship. Even in that limited corral, the reader will find as many defini-tions of what it means to bless as there are writers on the subject, so the one I offer below will not unduly burden discourse. On the issue that concerns us here, specifically blessing relationships along with the people in them, the leaders of the Claiming the Blessing movement have proposed a multilevel definition, which sees in the speech act of blessing a word about creation and about relation-ships, divine and human: "When the Church chooses 'to bless' something it is declaring that this particular person or persons or thing is a gift/blessing from God and his/her/its/their purpose is to live in (or, in the case of things, to assist in) covenanted re-lationship with God (and with all creation), i.e., to bless God in return."[3] While that prose is perhaps a bit daunting, its meaning is not irretrievable, and it restores to our thinking the idea that blessing changes the perception and function of its object, an idea

---

3. www.integrityusa.org/voice/2003/Winter2003.pdf.

that eluded the liturgical reformers of the 1960s who would do no more than give thanks by way of blessing. As a seventeenth-century lay theologian reminded his anxious puritan neighbors, "Blessing is made with thanksgiving, not by it."

In Greek, the language in which Christian theology was formed, the idea of "speaking good/well" (the Greek word we translate "bless") is a very active verb. The Hebrew mind could not separate words and things: Isaac could not take back Jacob's blessing and give it to Esau because the word-event of blessing had been accomplished. As the Hebrew and Greek backgrounds met, the idea arose that if God speaks well of something, if God calls it good, that is what it is, and the discussion is over as to the consequences. Hence to pronounce God's blessing is to say a creative and sanctifying word that something or someone is or is to function for the good, regardless of appearances.

Blessing makes something holy, that is, devoted to God. Thus our new perception of the person, thing, or relationship blessed provides it with a new "set apart" identity and gives it focused purpose. Making a relationship holy is to assign it divine purpose or surrender it to divine use. To bless the day-in-day-out commitment of a human couple, with all its relational modulations, reorders perception of what may be devoted to God (holy), and the thoroughgoing pervenience of divine grace.

To bless something in this sense is to speak well of it in terms of how it is perceived, what meaning it bears, what purpose it serves. Therefore that which is blessed becomes a symbol, in the highest sense. In Paul Tillich's familiar terms, a symbol is different from a sign (which gives only information) in that a symbol shares in, or is a part of, a greater reality while it points to it. We might even say that a symbol conveys a reality beyond itself. Eucharistic bread is not "just" a symbol. It is a symbol in the fullest and very best sense of the word. That is to say, regarding relationships, that the blessed union is to be not only a reminder of the kind of love Christ has for the church, but will, the rites pray, bear that love to the parties and to those with whom they interact.

Besides the reordering of perceptions, the setting aside for a new identity that is devoted to God and effects God's purpose, the blessing of persons, things, and relationships in the Bible and the tradition also invokes divine preservation and favor. Here is where the fear of magic is most agitated, and agitation and fear are the enemies of imagination. In the first place, secular investigators into the measurable effects of prayer as well as those who theologize from quantum physics increasingly invite us to abandon the Newtonian fundamentalism that minimizes what is conventionally called the "power of prayer" and look at prayer as a means of entering realms not obvious to old science. But that is not the chief point. People pray for the dead in part because their continuing love and care for the deceased must be expressed, and also because God is understood to invite humanity to bring all that is on our hearts to prayer. Similarly a blessing is asked on food not because anyone still believes that saying grace prevents botulism, but because of the human need to hear ourselves acknowledge our dependence on that which we cannot make, and because that acknowledgment produces the kind of thanksgiving that comes from humble hearts. That does indeed change the nature of eating and the perception of what is eaten; blessing food is an act of signal significance, much like that of blessing a couple's relationship. Along with the widely varying understanding of how God acts in history, prayer for preservation for people, things, and relationships emanates from the heart's desire, and as such must be brought to God.

To bless a relationship is both to recognize its inherent sacredness and to set it apart, to place it among the eternal cloud of holy things and people that surround us. Such an act makes it a symbol, that which announces and participates in a sacred meaning; it is also to invoke divine protection as the relationship does its work of bearing grace. This is what the bishops' committee meant in reporting that the rites for blessing unions saw themselves as "sacramental marriage," or what Gray Temple means when he argues for "sacramental equality." The liturgical tradition speaks of marriage, following Ephesians, as a symbol of Christ's love for the church. Such symbolism is not understood to be "just" a reminder, but is understood to be a participation in the kind of love Christ has for the church: giving, sustaining, nourishing, guiding. As every priest who has explained the marriage service to those preparing for their wedding has undoubtedly said, even the most secularized couple who try to convey and live those four values in their marriage soon find that they are dealing with ultimate questions, questions of theology.

Finally, for those who believe that God acts, blessing does more than to reorder perceptions: it invites and beseeches God to act for the sake of the persons united and for the sake of all whom they will touch in their life together.

To sum up and propose a working definition: to bless a union is to ask God to make it an experience of the kind and intensity of Christ's love, both for the couple and also for all who are touched by their life together. Thus blessing a union is not to wish it good fortune or merely to give thanks for it, although both certainly occur: it is to set it aside for a holy use, to perceive it to be grace-bearing, to *expect* God to use it. Thus the question about the appropriateness of the blessing of same-sex marriages is this question: Can the relationship between two people giving themselves to each other for life participate in and convey to others the love of the self-giving Christ? How one answers that question has profound impact on how one approaches the question of the blessing of any kind of union. Liturgies for blessing same-sex unions, then, tend both to bless and also to affirm the rightness of blessing. Because this is an unresolved and at times painful question for the church, some of the liturgies are slightly argumentative in their opening section — precisely as Cranmer was in claiming that opposite-sex marriage was an estate just as good as monastic profession.

A question is also being raised about blessing other sexual unions (hetero- or homosexual) that do not involve this commitment to a life of growing together with Christlike commitment.

All that can be observed here is that if the parties want a liturgy to mark "going steady," it must necessarily be set out in terms quite different than those of marriage rites, and the few rites that celebrate such an event are quite careful to draw distinctions. The same might be said for rites marking an "engagement," although there the goal is focused on people moving toward the state of permanent commitment.

In the heterosexual marriage rite the Reformers inherited, the Blessing of the Couple had become almost entirely a blessing of the bride, hoping for her to have the blessings of fecundity and fidelity, both in great measure. The husband was more or less left to do as he pleased, and there is evidence that he often did. Cranmer recast this in more equitable terms, and some of his words remain in the Blessing of the Couple in the 1979 Prayer Book, the text that is the basis for many of the same-sex rites. The blessing is in two parts. The first part is a choice between two sections of what was an entire blessing in the 1928 book.

> Most gracious God, we give you thanks for your tender love in sending Jesus Christ to come among us, to be born of a human mother, and to make the way of the cross to be the way of life. We thank you, also, for consecrating the union of man and woman in his Name. By the power of your Holy Spirit, pour out the abundance of your blessing upon this man and this woman. Defend them from every enemy. Lead them in all peace. Let their love for each other be a seal upon their hearts, a mantle about their shoulders, and a crown upon their foreheads. Bless them in their work and in their companionship; in their sleeping and in their waking; in their joys and in their sorrows; in their life and in their death. Finally, in your mercy, bring them to that table where your saints feast for ever in your heavenly home; through Jesus Christ our Lord, who with you and the Holy Spirit lives and reigns, one God, for ever and ever. *Amen.*

or

> O God, you have so consecrated the covenant of marriage that in it is represented the spiritual unity between Christ and his

Church: Send therefore your blessing upon these your servants, that they may so love, honor, and cherish each other in faithfulness and patience, in wisdom and true godliness, that their home may be a haven of blessing and peace; through Jesus Christ our Lord, who lives and reigns with you and the Holy Spirit, one God, now and for ever. *Amen.*

For purposes of blessing a same-sex couple, either form needs adjustment, of course, but there is a larger question. The first passage is long, but rich in image and allusion. The second is shorter, but matter-of-fact and more abstractly theological. No matter which of these paragraphs is chosen, the Prayer Book blessing concludes:

God the Father, God the Son, God the Holy Spirit, bless, preserve, and keep you; the Lord mercifully with his favor look upon you, and fill you with all spiritual benediction and grace; that you may faithfully live together in this life, and in the age to come have life everlasting. *Amen.*

This second section is rarely altered in same-sex rites. The first section has been adapted by the majority of local and diocesan liturgies to read:

Most gracious God, we give you thanks for your tender love in sending Jesus Christ to come among us, to be born of a human mother, and to make the way of the cross the way of life. By the power of your Holy Spirit, pour out the abundance of your blessing upon these persons. Defend them from every enemy, etc.

At All Saints, Pasadena, this last paragraph is the entire blessing; the California liturgy goes on, as do the rites at St. Thomas and the original New Westminster, to the Trinitarian blessing. The second New Westminster rite does not contain a Trinitarian blessing.

Anne and Brenda's service reflects the minority option, with the Prayer Book's second paragraph adapted to read:

O God, lover of humankind, in whom all our covenants are established, send your blessing upon your servants Anne and

Brenda, that they may so love, honor, and cherish each other in faithfulness and patience, in wisdom and true godliness, etc.

This blessing then goes on to the final paragraph as printed in the Prayer Book.

The Second Consultation took a fresh look at the blessing. Its text follows the form of Jewish table graces, considered by many to have been determinative of the shape of early Christian eucharistic prayers. Those Jewish texts praise and thank God for creation and salvation, and move to a supplication for blessing with a final doxology. We find just this form in the Consultation's blessing. It begins with praise and thanks in just those words:

> Praise and thanks to you, O God,
> Creator and sustainer of the world.
> You spoke and the heavens came into being,
> The earth and everything that lives.
> You looked and found it good.
> The world was charged with your glory and mercy.
> Praise and thanks to you, O God,
> Liberator and Healer of the world.
> You have broken down the world of division,
> Calling together by the law of love those who were apart.
> For this Christ died, giving birth to a new creation.
> Praise and thanks to you, Lord our God.
> You renew the face of the earth.
> Pour out your Holy Spirit upon N. and N.
> Let them love each other openly without fear,
> A joyful sign of your new creation in justice, love and peace.

Deacon   People of God, give praise to God.
People   Blessed be God who appears to us in their love.

The much-repeated antiphon aside, it might be observed that of all the texts for blessings, this one gives the couple the least attention — but it might well be argued that it does the best job of situating their union within God's work of creation and redemption. The one presiding continues:

The living God bless you.
May you flourish together
And rejoice in your friends.
[May God bless your children.]
May God grant you the goods that endure
And bring you everlasting joy.
And the blessing of the Living God,
The Source, the Word and the Spirit,
Be upon you now and forever. *Amen.*

A question that only time can settle is whether in celebrating something as concrete and intimate as the union of two persons it is appropriate or helpful to name God in a way that is cerebral, impersonal, and ultimately *not a name* in the way that Abba is. One cannot help but hear "The Force" of *Star Wars* fame in its rhyme, "The Source," a fact that by itself suggests further work.

It seems that in terms of what the Claiming the Blessing movement looks for in a blessing, each of the forms reviewed addresses some points, but none satisfies all of them. In every case, however, it seems that the identification of the relationship as arena of grace-filled activity and source of blessing to others is touched upon in the Prayers of the People that precede the Blessing proper.

In the ritual masses of the Prayer Book, ordination excepted, the Prayers of the People are for the most part for and about the candidates, and this is true of the 1979 marriage service (pp. 429f.). The prayers address the interpersonal relating of the couple and the effect it will have on the world. This is the pattern the same-sex rites generally follow, although the Consultation liturgy, consistent with the wide range of topics addressed in its blessing, gives more time to general intercession in its prayers. Anne and Brenda mixed the marriage prayers with general intercessions, as we have seen. A similar mixed form is found in the service at St. Thomas, Washington. The 2004 Washington diocesan rite also contains two hybrid intercessions, and permits any other forms of Prayers of the People in the Prayer Book or conforming to its directions. The first New Westminster rite provides the Prayer Book texts with only the slightest adaptation, but also provides alternatives, including the Consultation prayers and a set of intercessions prayed by family members, but the second Canadian rite has very little praying at all. The Glenn Dale rite shows the briefest set of intercessions, followed by the blessing from the Consultation. The Prayer Book form is used in some liturgies at All Saints, Pasadena, but there have also been prayers created for a particular occasion. In any event, these prayers must be considered with the blessings to see a complete picture of the couple's life in the parish and world.

Chapter Five

A Word and The Word

The cultural stereotype of a wedding, reinforced by film and soap operas alike, is that someone starts speaking at about an augmented fourth below the pitch of the normal speaking voice, beginning with the words, "Dearly Beloved," and the camera begins to pull back. This form of opening address is a particularly Anglican contribution to nuptial rites, and since the Reformation it has spread to a number of Protestant groups. However, the majority of the world's Christians are joined in rites that have no fixed opening address in this sense.

A number of the Episcopal same-sex rites also include an opening address, occasionally even beginning "Dearly Beloved." Many, like the following passage, compress the parallel passage in the Prayer Book:

> Beloved people of God: We have come together in the presence of God to witness and bless the covenant of love and fidelity which N. and N. have made with each other. The union of two persons in heart, body, and mind is intended by God for their mutual joy; for the help and comfort given one another in prosperity and adversity; and when it is God's will, for the procreation of children and their nurture in the knowledge and love of the Lord....

The issue of children is, of course, one that not even opposite-sex couples agree upon, and we have seen that there are other views of the "generative" aspects of all relationships. One of them is expressed in a same-sex rite of unknown provenance:

... for their mutual joy ... in prosperity and adversity ... and for the bringing forth of new life in Christ and the nurturance of others in the knowledge and love of the Lord.

Another issue that the use of a "Dearly Beloved" section raises is the question of what we have come here to do. Most rites that retain such a section mention the witnessing and blessing, and move on. Other writers have felt that this is a moment where a witness about the rightness of the liturgy must be made. Thus in one rite we read after the paragraph about the purpose and goods of holy union:

> We acknowledge that this union cannot yet be recognized as a legal "marriage" in the eyes of the state, or much of the Church. Nonetheless, we who are gathered here in celebration and support of this union believe that it *is* binding in the eyes of God, that it exemplifies the love between Christ and the Church, and that it is a prophetic witness to all, both within and without the Church. Our intent is to redeem the word [marriage] both for those to whom it has been denied and for those who have taken it too lightly.

Another rite begins this section by affirming that this union also fulfills God's purpose for humanity (that individuality be complemented), adding that "Christian compassion" presses the church to affirm all human couples. It then also adopts a somewhat prophetic voice:

> At this point in history, the Episcopal Church does not corporately and officially share that belief with regard to lesbian and gay unions, and so it is not possible for us to bless them formally for the Church. Nevertheless, we have come together here so that N. and N. may formally declare, in the presence of God and before the Church and the world, their commitment to one another in a sacred, binding covenant. By tradition and theological precept, couples are themselves the ministers of their covenants. The Church celebrates and affirms what already exists.

The Word of God

The Dearly Beloved address in Cranmer's 1549 rite had a distinct teaching purpose, for it was the only moment of instruction until the sermon on "the office of man and wife" (or his set of special supplemental readings) was delivered at the Eucharist following the marriage. The wedding itself needed no word liturgy, for one was to follow at the Eucharist. Cranmer's imagined pattern did not survive, and weddings generally did not take place before the Sunday liturgy, with the result that for much of Anglican history, scripture was not read at marriages. That has changed, and even if for some reason the Eucharist is not to be celebrated, the scriptures are to be proclaimed as both teaching and celebration in the Prayer Book rite.

The original New Westminster same-sex rite did not include a selection of lessons, but the other model rites do, and the second Canadian rite now includes a lectionary. In the United States, the selection of readings that reflects the least continuity with the Prayer Book is in the suggested Old Testament readings, and the most continuity in the passages recommended from the Gospels. The passages omitted from the Prayer Book suggestions are, of course, those that deal specifically with the details of opposite-sex marriage.

The only Old Testament lesson that is common to the Prayer Book and the same-sex specimen rites is Song of Solomon 2:10–13 (Many waters cannot quench love). In terms of commitment between persons of the same sex, although not universally thought to be sexual, the Consultation liturgy adds the possibilities of Jonathan and David's covenant (1 Sam. 18:1b, 3; 20:16–17), and Ruth's nonsexual commitment to her mother-in-law, Naomi (Ruth 1:16–17). Also suggested by the Consultation is Ecclesiastes 4:9–12, which begins, "Two are better than one," and which includes the verse, "Again, if two lie together, they keep warm; but how can one keep warm alone?" We have already noted Anne and Brenda's reading from Wisdom (8:6–10). St. Thomas in Washington suggests, in addition to the Consultation texts, Zephaniah 3:14–20 concerning the return of the exiled and outcast, and Micah 4:1–3, 6–8, with its hope that in the great coming day, all the people, even the injured and oppressed, will be called to Zion. The second New Westminster rite adds additional readings from the Song of Solomon (the seeking of the beloved in the night, and "set me as a seal on your heart").

A composite list of First Readings would then be:

Song of Solomon 2:10–13
Song of Solomon 3:1–4
Song of Solomon 8:6–7
1 Samuel 18:1b, 3; 20:16–17
Ruth 1:16–17
Ecclesiastes 4:9–12
Wisdom 8:6–10
Zephaniah 3:14–20
Micah 4:1–3, 6–10

The two prophetic notes of restoration and fulfillment despite oppression are echoed in the All Saints, Pasadena, suggestion of Romans 12:14–18, with its call to the persecuted to invoke blessings on one's persecutors. The passage as its stands in the liturgy seems to address the couple's function in the community in general:

Bless those who persecute you; bless and do not curse them. Rejoice with those who rejoice, weep with those who weep. Live in harmony with one another; do not be haughty, but associate with the lowly; do not claim to be wiser than you are. Do not repay anyone evil for evil, but take thought for what is noble in the sight of all. If it is possible, so far as it depends on you, live peaceably with all.

The Epistle lessons that the same-sex rites have in common with the Prayer Book are the "love chapter," of 1 Corinthians 13:1–13, and Colossians 3:12–17, concerning "love which binds together everything in harmony." The passage from 1 Corinthians 13 is the most commonly used in all the individual same-sex blessing service folders in the collection of the liturgical office, as it is in most opposite-sex weddings of which I have knowledge. Also in common is 1 John 4:7–16, "beloved, let us love one another." This passage links loving to Christ's identity and work in a way as powerful as the Ephesians reference to marriage, as signifying the relation of Christ and church, and may in some sense be considered its functional equivalent. The Consultation adds Romans 12:9–21 (Let love be genuine). St. Thomas adds 2 Corinthians 5:17–20 (If anyone is in Christ, there is a new creation). To this list the new New Westminster rite adds Galatians 5:13–14, 22–26 (servants to one another and fruits of the Spirit); Ephesians 4:25–27, 29–32 (be kind to one another); and 1 John 3:18–24 (love in truth and action).

The composite list of Second Readings would be:

Romans 12:14–18
1 Corinthians 13:1–13
2 Corinthians 5:17–20
Galatians 5:13–14, 22–26
Ephesians 4:25–27, 29–32
Colossians 3:12–17
1 John 3:18–24
1 John 4:7–16

The Prayer Book suggests Gospel readings from Matthew 5, one the Beatitudes passage (1–10) and the other the "Let your light so shine" of verses 13–16. Also suggested are Mathew 7:21, 24–29 (the house built on a rock) and John 15:9–12 (Love one another as I have loved you). The only Prayer Book suggestion not carried over in the same-sex liturgies is Mark 10:6–9, 13–16, the passage regarding creation, marriage, and divorce. That lesson includes the command, "What God has joined together let no one put asunder." While the passage is not among the suggested Gospel readings, a number of the liturgies include the command not to separate those joined by God, placing same-sex couples under the same protection as their opposite-sex counterparts. The Consultation and others add some of Luke's version of the Beatitudes (6:20–23), with their stronger emphasis on ultimate vindication of the persecuted and the laughter that will ultimately be theirs. To this St. Thomas adds Luke 6:32–38, about loving the enemy and withholding judgment on others. St. Thomas also adds John 2:1–11, the wedding at Cana, the sole reference to conventional marriage among the readings, although the emphasis is (as in the conventional applications) on Jesus' providing for the festivities through the sign of changing water into wine. The second New Westminster rite adds John 17:1, 18–26 (that the world may see).

A composite list of Gospels then is:

Matthew 5:1–10
Matthew 5:13–16
Matthew 7:21, 24–29
Luke 6:20–23
Luke 6:32–38
John 2:1–11
John 15:9–12
John 17:1, 18–26

The 2004 Washington rite and the second New Westminster rite both contain almost all the lessons from the composite list.

Other Readings

One does hear reports of exotic readings from bizarre, even outrageous, secular sources being used at same-sex celebrations. I have found no evidence to support such claims.

A number of the services examined do indeed include provisions for readings from sources other than the Bible. This provision is not uncommon in weddings performed with the Prayer Book rite, and the use of additional readings is all but assumed by the Prayer Book's Order for Marriage (a "Rite III" service, p. 435).

Readings from sources outside the scriptures follow no evident pattern other than their meaningfulness to the parties. In some cases poetry written for the occasion by family members or friends is read. A 1997 rite drew on a mixture of Native American wisdom, English mystics, and contemporary writers. The reading of mystics along with the scriptures is not uncommon in the liturgies from All Saints, Pasadena. Several services there and elsewhere read from Aelred of Rievaulx (1110–67), whose *Mirror of Love* and *Spiritual Friendship* are widely known. From *Spiritual Friendship* (based on Cicero's essay on friendship) this passage has been used in a number of union services:

> One is entirely alone without a friend. But what happiness, what security, what joy to have someone to whom you dare to speak on terms of equality as to another self; one to whom you need have no fear to confess all of your failings; one to whom you can unblushingly make known what progress you have made in the spiritual life; one to whom you can entrust all the secrets of your heart and before whom you can place all your plans. What, therefore, is more pleasant than so to unite to oneself the spirit of another and the two form one, that no boasting is thereafter to be feared, no suspicion to be dreaded, no correction of one by the other to cause pain, no praise on the part of one to bring a change of adulation from the other.

None of the rites examined include at this point what might be considered polemic or justification for what is taking place. Each reading seeks to build or celebrate the relationship, as it would in conventional services uniting a couple. It is for others to identify the sources of reports to the contrary.

Chapter Six

Vows and Tokens

I t is in the making of vows that union liturgies come to their clearest focus; the couple are themselves traditionally spoken of as the ministers of this exchange. The vows in the Prayer Book marriage service have really changed very little from the Cranmerian form of 1549:

> I N. take thee N. to my wedded wife/husband, to have and to holde from this day forwarde, for better, for wurse, for richer, for poorer, in sickenes, and in health, to love and to cherishe, til death us departe: according to Goddes holy ordeinaunce: And therto I plight thee my trouth.

That formula boils down to taking the other as beloved spouse for all time and in all circumstances (to "plight troth" is to promise truth or faithfulness). There is something to be said for the ordinariness of these words: their meaning is unmistakable.

Similarly, the vows in the Consultation liturgy, also in a short dialogue form, are clear and uncomplicated. Each party ends up having said to the other:

> I give myself to you. I take you to have and to hold from this day forward, to love and to cherish, for better or worse, in sickness and in health, as my companion, lover, and friend. This is my solemn vow.

All Saints, Pasadena, usually follows this pattern, although words vary slightly, as do those at St. George's in Glenn Dale.

The practice of some same-sex couples who refer to each other as husbands or wives has not had an effect on those producing liturgies, and no liturgy to come under my lens contains husband or wife language. The avoidance of that vocabulary has led to the search for words that are perhaps richer, as in the expression "companion, lover, and friend," words that also reflect the evolution of the relatively recent development of "companionate marriage" in the culture in general.

On the other hand, we have seen Brenda and Anne make vows in which no relationship is specifically named. Again, each of them vowed:

> I promise you, N., to honor and cherish you in life's joys and triumphs and to stand with you in times of grief and misfortune. I will be truthful in all things and strive with you to create a home filled with reverence and hospitality. I promise to love you all the days of my life.

They reserve the naming of relationship for the giving of the rings, where each denominates the other "my friend, my sister, my partner, my spouse."

Some of the orders examined provide for each partner to write a vow. New Westminster (both versions) is among those where the relationship is not named, but the commitments are named creatively:

> I give myself to you. I love you, I trust you, I delight in you. I will bear your burdens, I will share your joys, and I will go with you wherever God calls us. This is my solemn vow.

St. Thomas in Washington does not name a relationship in the vows or the giving of tokens, but again evokes more detail in the not-naming:

> N., I join my life with yours, from this day forward. In prosperity and in hardship, in health and in sickness, in joy and in sorrow, I will love, protect and support you as long as we both shall live. This I vow before God.

Those vows that do follow the Consultation pattern do not state the "till death do us part" promise expressly, although some others do, and one may infer the intention from the language used in New Westminster. Certainly no rite explicitly excludes the sentiment, but this may be a point that fuels further discussion.

In the ancient world, covenants were marked by some sign or token, so one can understand that the emphasis on covenanting in both opposite- and same-sex rites would heighten the emphasis on symbolic gifts. The Prayer Book provides for tokens other than a ring, and a number of the same-sex rites do that as well.

Moderns may have difficulty remembering that the wearing of rings by both partners in opposite-sex unions has been a practice that has not been consistently followed, and that a few generations ago a "double ring" ceremony was remarkable. In part this fact reflects the old assumption that only the male partner could meaningfully say, "With all my worldly goods I thee endow," hogwash as it occasionally was, as often the husband had a great deal to gain by a wedding and in any event owned all of his wife's property from the moment of their marriage. The present Prayer Book formula includes here, "with all that I have, I honor you," which is not quite the same thing, if one is disposed to look for loopholes. In times when the legal and cultural definitions of how one shares resources in lifelong relationships are in flux, there is perhaps wisdom in the reticence of the new rites on the subject of property.

Other Ritual Elements

The most widely noted addition to the familiar rites is the rather dramatic ceremony of "crowning the couple" in the Consultation rite, an element borrowed from the Byzantine liturgy (by way, it seems, of a decade's use in Boston). The Consultation rite also provides that they may also be anointed, tied with a cord, or draped in a mantle or humeral veil. One wonders if the latter practice is meant to reflect the reference in the Song of Songs to being under the banner of love. Also provided for is the leading of the couple around the altar, the action that follows the crowning in the Byzantine rite. The traditional Byzantine texts follow the very lengthy crowning rite with a long chant that includes various petitions in the form of "bless them as you blessed..." — usually concluding each petition with the naming of a married couple, from Abraham and Sarah through Zechariah and Elizabeth. Among the pairs additionally named in the Consultation version are Ruth and Naomi and David and Jonathan.

What is even more eye-catching about this chant is that it preserves the stark realism of the Byzantine text from which it is excerpted by also taking the verses that indicate that a life together may be very demanding: "Preserve them as you did Noah in the ark...Jonah in the belly of the whale...the Holy Children in the fiery furnace," adding on their own, "...as you preserved Jesus in the tomb."

Chapter Seven

Holy Communion

C elebrating a ritual mass may in some cases have been
thought of as a way to obtain the fruits generated
by the eucharistic sacrifice for those who had been
baptized, confirmed, or married, etc. As the eucharistic Preface in
those celebrations makes clear, there is still some sense of "special
intention" for those whose lives have been marked by the just-
concluded ritual.

Even absent notions of special intention at the Eucharist, there
are differences in the celebration upon these occasions. The most
important is to observe that putting the particular sacrament or
other rite being celebrated within the eucharistic context is to sit-
uate it within the celebration of creation, the gift of Christ to the
world, the central acts of our salvation, and the reception of the
graces of the Holy Communion for both power and purpose in
living. In other words, the events of the day are placed in clos-
est proximity to the celebration of creation and redemption: our
moving them into the neighborhood of our chief act of worship
is in itself to bless, to speak well, of them. The Proper Preface
and Postcommunion Prayers at such celebrations express how the
day's celebration of the Eucharist and reception of Holy Communion relate to the particular concerns of the gathering, bringing it
into eucharistic focus.

Speaking as a liturgist, it is here that I find the present rites
for blessing same-sex unions less than complete. The Consultation
assumes the Preface for the day. Brenda and Anne used the Preface
for the Ascension. New Westminster provides no proper preface,
but does have an offertory prayer:

> God of the covenant, hear our prayer, and accept all we offer you this day. May the mystery of Christ's unselfish love, which we celebrate in this Eucharist, increase our love for you and for each other, through Christ our Lord.

In the second rite, this becomes:

> Faithful God, with these gifts you offer us communion in your Servant, Jesus Christ. May we who celebrate this sacrament be filled with the same self-offering love made manifest in him. This we ask in Christ's name.

A number of All Saints, Pasadena, liturgies omit a proper preface altogether, particularly those using a Rite One Eucharist. Several others at All Saints use a contemporary eucharistic prayer whose preface is not actually about the union of couples, but does shed light:

> ... Through us you move, and through us you are made known to the world. Co-creators with you, we are emboldened to move beyond ourselves, to find the courage to let go of old ways and to welcome new life. And so ...

One liturgy based on the Consultation rite uses the Preface of Baptism. The California rite has created a preface, however:

> You created us to share in your divine life, and forming us in your image you called us to live in harmony with you and all creation in your Kingdom; through the unity of persons one with another, you teach us that love is our origin, our constant calling, and our fulfillment in heaven.

St. Thomas Parish in Washington remains close to traditional wording in its Preface:

> Because in the holy covenant of love between two people You have given us an image of the heavenly Jerusalem where we will be finally united with Your Son Jesus Christ our Lord; who loves us and gave himself for us to make the whole creation new....

One preface, in a liturgy designed to recognize Jewish tradition as well as Christian, included this:

We praise you and bless you, O holy and living God, through whom we find our center and shalom. You are the light that invites us out of ourselves into connection and commitment to another. You are the spirit that blesses N. and N. and gives them the strength for their life's journey together.

Remembering that the St. Thomas liturgy is to serve both same- and opposite-sex couples, one is not surprised to find a multi-use postcommunion prayer, again derived from the Prayer Book text:

> ...We give You thanks for binding us together in these holy mysteries of the Body and Blood of Your Son Jesus Christ. Grant that by Your Holy Spirit, N. and N., now joined in marriage/holy union, may become one in heart and soul....

While such a provision recognizes legal realities, it also gives participants perhaps more of an opportunity to decide what they in fact will call their relationship. The Consultation itself sets forth neither preface nor postcommunion prayer, providing only that the couple may wish to bear the oblations, and with the permission of the ordinary, administer the chalice at communion.

All Saints, Pasadena, in one of its texts, takes the Prayer Book postcommunion prayer and simply omits the words I have bracketed below:

> O God, the giver of all that is true and lovely and gracious: We give you thanks for binding us together in these holy mysteries of the Body and Blood of your Son Jesus Christ. Grant that by your Holy Spirit, N. and N. [now joined in Holy Matrimony,] may become one in heart and soul, live in fidelity and peace, and obtain those eternal joys prepared for all who love you; for the sake of Jesus Christ our Lord. *Amen.*

Another All Saints liturgy uses "now joined in holy covenant" in the bracketed place, where the California service has "in solemn covenant," an expression that can be found in individual service folders in the early 1990s.

Where St. Thomas levels the praying field upward by including the name for each relationship, All Saints levels down by not naming the category of relationship.

Only a very few of the rites examined anticipate that the celebration of the Eucharist does not take place.

Chapter Eight

Not Unadvisedly or Lightly

The Couple and the Parish

The inquiry here is pastoral as well as liturgical, and it is noteworthy that considerable attention has been paid by those proposing rites for blessing same-sex couples to the insistence that pastoral care be ample.

The Consultation document has a detailed plan, so we turn first to its provisions. The consultants devote energy to the attitudes and beliefs of the parish, its clergy, and its bishop as creating the matrix in which the rite is celebrated. The consulting authors believed strongly that clergy must not act alone in this matter, but in conversation with parish and bishop.

Such a background makes it natural, they believe, that as a couple is prepared for the first such celebration in the parish, *the catechesis extends to the entire parish.* For this reason, the Consultation, like others who have considered the subject, seeks congregational sponsors to accompany couples preparing for either opposite- or same-sex commitments. Clearly the latter category requires the greater attention, because societal and ecclesiastical support is scarcer for same-sex couples.

The sponsors would follow the couple from the early stages of their forming the intent to unite, assisting and accompanying them as they examined the promises they would be making and considered their impact on the remainder of their life.

The Consultation also suggests that each parish have a plan for how it teaches children about what is happening around them.

Especially as its proposed rite takes place at the Sunday Eucharist, this would seem to be a necessary step, as is their reminder that ministry to gay and lesbian adolescents cannot but be affected by a parish's decision to celebrate the rite.

From my encounters with clergy and couples in preparation for writing this essay, it seems that the preliturgy pastoral counseling is very much the same as it would be for other couples. They are asked to plan the liturgy, be up-to-date in health and legal matters, have a financial plan for how they will live together, and establish some skills for discussing their life and its issues. They are asked then, and partially through the more preliminary-appearing concerns, to begin to know the spiritual values of a committed life and what they have to do with the power of God in Christ. A number of couples have emphasized the importance of supporters through the process; others did not bring it up until asked. Naturally there arose the special concerns of being a same-sex couple when the majority view in our culture is not supportive. What is significant is the number of couples who reported this conversation in terms of its leading to their commitment to support others, rather than an increased need for support for themselves.

In the Diocese of Bethlehem, the Safe Spaces Committee formed in response to the General Convention of 2000 has produced a syllabus for preunion counseling. It is particularly the work of the Reverend Jane Williams, Ph.D., and Rita Valenti, Ph.D., both licensed psychologists and members of the diocese. I reproduce their syllabus here in its current provisional form of August 2004. The committee intends to do much more work on the project, but it indicates a way of addressing the pastoral issues.

They write: "Clergy who counsel a gay, lesbian, or transgendered (GLT) couple seeking a blessing ceremony need to be aware of a variety of issues that differentiate GLT couples from heterosexual couples. Prior to engaging in pre-blessing counseling, clergy should become aware of and comfortable discussing such things as:

- specific differences in the role of relationship in the GLT community as opposed to the heterosexual community; specific cultural differences in the role of relationship and sexuality in the gay and the lesbian community

- legal issues that must be addressed by GLT couples to enable sharing of property, inheritance rights, adoption, medical decision-making, etc.

- lack of cultural role models and societal support for GLT couplehood

- difficulties and ambiguities in negotiating the process of "coming out" to different social groups (parents, partners' parents, workplace, children, church community, etc.)

- differences in the role of previous relationships and sexual contacts in the GLT community as opposed to the heterosexual community (and subtle differences between gay couples and lesbian couples)

- the role of church and scripture as sources of internal conflict re: sexual identity rather than a resource or source of support

"To develop such awarenesses and skills in dealing with them, clergy may decide to participate in a Diocesan-based training group, form a colleague support/supervision group, and/or avail themselves of a variety of written resources to be made available through Diocesan House as an annotated bibliography. Additionally, legal and counseling resources will be identified by Diocesan House and names made available to clergy on request.

"Issues to be addressed in Pre-Blessing Counseling should include, but not be restricted to the following:

1. What is the couple's definition/understanding of their couple-ness and their commitment? (among the concerns here are differences of GLT and heterosexual culture and consequent expectations and norms of relationships; legal issues involved in assuring partner access to medical decisions, end of life issues, transfers/sharing of property, etc.)

2. What is the meaning of the Blessing of the Union ceremony to this couple? What is the significance of a spiritually based ceremony to them? (is this ceremony intended to make their relationship "official"? to provide a witness to others? to confirm their relationship

in a way meaningful to them? other?) What is the role of spirituality for them, singly and as a couple?

3. What has been each partner's relationship history? How have previous relationships functioned? What role do previous relationships play in the current relationship and friendship circle? (Clergy should note that in gay relationships, previous partners/lovers are frequently part of the current relationship as friends or in other roles; differences exist in the role of previous partners in the current relationships of gay men and lesbians.)

4. What has been the process of identity formation and how "out" are each of the partners in the couple? (who knows? who doesn't? how does the couple negotiate their world of work, social connections, family?)

5. Are there children? How will they be integrated into this new family? How does the couple cope with the children's acceptance or non-acceptance of the new relationship? If there are no children, does the couple intend to have children by one of the partners? adopt? Are there issues of regret or grief if they are childless?

6. How does the couple communicate with each other? Handle conflict? What are the family models of each partner for communication, conflict management, problem-solving, handling and expressing emotion? How do they decide such matters as finances, job changes/relocation, living arrangements, etc.?

7. What role does spirituality play in their relationship? What role does God play in their relationship? What image do they hold of God? What spiritual practices do they have as a couple? as individuals? What spiritual practices might they want to develop in their relationship? What is the role of the church community in their lives? Do they have expectations of the church community (positive or negative) in regard to their relationship and participation in the church community? What wounds do they carry (if any) from past interactions with churches, clergy, scripture, religiously identified individuals? What things would they want to give to the church (the clergyperson can make connections with specific people and groups in the church)?

8. How do they handle sexuality? What are the couple's boundaries with regard to sexuality? Are there functional sexual difficulties that they have coped with? not coped with? How? Are they both in

good health sexually? HIV-positive? How have they discussed their sexuality together?

9. Other issues (age differences and caretaking, financial responsibility of each partner, independence/interdependence/dependence, etc.)"

A great deal of the wisdom that Williams and Valenti distill here could inform the counseling of all couples as they approach the taking of spouses.

When Dioceses Decide

I guessed that the process leading up to a diocesan decision might have begun with a convention resolution or a bishop's address. This was not the case in the diocese I investigated in detail, Delaware. The diocesan convention resolution made a decision that was in fact the capstone on a six-year process, not its beginning. The origin of the process was not any agency or office on the diocesan level. It was the request of a number of parishes for assistance in their pastoral care of same-sex couples. The six years between the request and the decision were marked by study and conversation on every level of parish life and in all bodies in the diocese. The intention was that a decision be made based on "a coherent theological and liturgical position," and thus theological conversation was held around the issues of blessing, commitment, sacrament, and the relation of these blessings to other rites. Also consulted formally were same-sex couples who had been living faithfully over the years; these interviews convinced the inquirers that the relationships were in fact grace-generating for those in them.

Before proposing anything to their convention, those desiring the rite were also concerned that its integrity be preserved just as would the integrity of conventional marriage. They did not want their diocese to become a marriage mill for couples from surrounding territory, and they did not want to create another category of "Marrying Sam(antha)" among the clergy. The rite was to be understood as that of the church for its faithful, so the adoption of the position by the convention involved some limitations as well as permissions.

The initial standards provide for the pastoral care of the couple and the integrity of the community:

A. Blessing same-gender relationships, like other pastoral ministries, is a congregational ministry. The bishop is ready to support this ministry in congregations only where an educational process has been carried out and where there is substantial agreement among congregational leaders.

B. At least one member of the couple being blessed must be an active member of the congregation where the blessing will take place.

C. The couple will receive significant counseling and pastoral preparation prior to the Service of Blessing. Part of this counseling will be a clear statement that this service is an ecclesiastical act. It does not convey legal or contractual rights in the State.

D. Inappropriate media attention has the potential to stir up unnecessary conflict and detract from the pastoral nature of this ministry. The bishop's office will provide consultation to a congregation and a spokesperson to whom the media should be referred for questions, interviews, etc.

E. If a non-parochial priest is asked to participate in a Service of Blessing, the priest will refer the couple to a congregation in the diocese where this ministry is being practiced. Non-parochial clergy may assist in a Service of Blessing when invited by the congregational leadership.

F. Clergy from other Episcopal dioceses may not be invited to assist without the written permission of their bishop. Clergy from other denominations may not be invited to assist without the written permission of their judicatory head.

G. The bishop will provide an outline for the Service of Blessing and samples of suggested wording of the service.

H. Services of Blessing should not be part of regularly scheduled worship on a Sunday or Holy Day.

The liturgy issued in that diocese is interesting for this study in terms of the address to the people, the vows, and the actual Blessing of the Couple. It reflects the influence of the Australian, rather than the New Zealand, Prayer Book, and seems not much influenced by American efforts. The address does not begin "Dearly Beloved," or with any other vocative, and avoids the Cranmerian pattern entirely:

> We are here, before God, to witness a solemn covenant, which N. and N. will make before us. We come as their family and friends to share their joy, to affirm them, and to pray for the Lord's blessing upon them now, and in their future.
>
> This is a Christian covenant. Every commitment made in Christ's name begins with the baptism of new birth. New life, given to us in the Risen One, leads the members of Christ's Body into many forms of committed living: to varieties of service and callings, to friendships shared along the way, for some, to vowed communities of special vocation, and for many, to hearing God's call in a lasting relationship of fidelity to one other person. Down through the ages, many have been called into committed relationships like the one we bless today.
>
> This covenant is spoken in public with an invitation to all to support it. This covenant in made in the community of faith where they have received regular nourishment in fellowship, prayer, and hope. This covenant is made in the Lord where there is stability for sharing longings and desires, power for encouragement, grace to forgive and accept forgiveness, strength to help in perplexity or fear, and depth and height to experience awe and joy in mutual discovery.

Consent is given to the questions, "Do you trust N.? Are you ready to enter a lifelong covenant with *him*? Will you stand by *him* forever no matter what life shall bring?" Again, despite the fine use of language, we return to a liturgy where the vows are in essence made twice, as is the case in the Prayer Book.

The vows meet some of the concerns we noted above about lifelong commitment: "N., in the mystery of Divine Love, I offer my life to you, mind, body, and spirit. I take you as my own in hope, joy, and peace. I promise all my strength for your well-being, and I pledge my loyalty to you all the days of my life." As in the case of Anne and Brenda's service, these vows seem to promise more, not less, than those in the Prayer Book.

After the ring (essentially the Prayer Book form) and the Prayers of the People (a fresh text, but with an antipodean fragrance) the celebrant joins the couple's hands and says,

> Now that N. and N. have spoken their vows before God and those present, and have given to each other signs of their commitment, their covenant is sealed. We now pray God's blessing on them.
>
> May the God of peace bless, preserve, and keep you, may God be gracious to you, guide you in truth and peace, and make you strong in love and faith, so that you may grow together in this life, and the love that you share be taken up beyond death itself, to dwell in God's eternal glory.

Setting aside the question that might be raised about an afterlife where none are given in marriage, one notes that this is the most compact of the blessings, and the one least dependent on Prayer Book texts.

There is an example of a diocese where the bishop led the way, Kansas, with subsequent ratification by diocesan convention through the failure of a vote to disassociate the convention from his action. Again, his action was taken after consultation in the diocese and in response to needs made known to him. The difference is that his directive has to do with *all* couples for whom marriage is impossible, opposite- as well as same-sex couples. His directives include blessings for "(1) heterosexual couples for whom Holy Matrimony would create a financial hardship due to loss of income resulting from marriage, and (2) homosexual partners."

While such a provision might lead one to liturgical conclusions like the dual-purpose rite from St. Thomas, Washington, D.C., noted above, in Kansas the bishop understood the blessing of this couple as something other than an equivalent of matrimony, at least in liturgical appearance. "The proposed rite for the blessing of the relationship shall not be considered to be Holy Matrimony, and shall be distinct from and in no way resemble 'The Celebration and Blessing of a Marriage' in the Book of Common Prayer or similar rites used in other traditions. Rites that may be suitable for adaptation can be found in The Book of Occasional Services (1994), including 'The Blessing of Homes at Easter' (99–102) or 'The Blessing of a Home' (146–156)."

The plan of the former bishop of Kansas, like that of the Diocese of Delaware, requires substantial agreement among parish leadership. The puzzle to the student of liturgy is why the liturgical provision is so slight when these blessings are limited to "those who commit to the standards the Church expects of Holy Matrimony, namely, 'living in other lifelong committed relationships' which are 'characterized by fidelity, monogamy, mutual affection and respect, careful, honest communication, and the holy love which enables those in such relationships to see in each other the image of God.'" Given these very high standards, one wonders why, once the decision to bless has been made, it would not be better to allow the couple to publicly promise these things to each other, an act that would indeed make the liturgy as marriage-like as are the standards imposed on the couple.

Like the previously observed diocesan plans, this one calls for parish membership by one of the persons seeking the blessing, and a program of pastoral care and preparation.

The diocesan policy adopted in Washington, D.C., in 2004 is very similar to the Delaware plan. One member of the couple must be a communicant in the diocese, and preblessing counseling is required. Clergy from outside the diocese must be licensed to preside at any blessing, and rectors of parishes remain in control of the use of parish facilities for any services. It is required that before a rite is celebrated the "clergy asked to officiate is to seek the advice and counsel of the vestry," but it is to be noted that their approval is not required.

The rite adopted in Washington is to be a Eucharist, but its model, according to its drafters, is not the marriage service, but the "Setting Apart for a Special Vocation" in the *Book of Occasional Services*. This point can be taken to the extent that the baptism is mentioned, that the address to the assembly concerns covenant-making, and that some of the prayers are vocationally oriented, but the service in the main has the look and feel of a service of union, and the last paragraph of the Blessing of the Couple is Cranmer's familiar nuptial blessing.

The reader is encouraged to go to the website of the Diocese of Vermont and read their forty-six-page document. There is no more thorough study and action plan currently available from a diocese. Taken together with the New York diocesan publication (also available online) *Let the Reader Understand*, it provides scriptural, theological, and practical study that is carefully researched and coherently argued.

The Vermont document studies the history of General Convention actions and the state of the conversation in the Anglican Communion. It then takes careful note of the Vermont context, as Vermont has had same-sex civil unions since 2000. Then follows a study of Anglican theological method and the theological topics that have to do with the blessings of union. The diocese takes the position found in the New Westminster position paper, that in pronouncing a blessing, the priest merely identifies something for what it already is. Nonetheless, the texts they set forth uniformly ask God to do something new. This anomaly is widespread, and if the church is to do something on a national level, it is a point where intense discussion can be anticipated.

After considering the pros and cons of taking action at this point in history, the commission appointed to study the issue concluded that the diocese had to risk moving ahead.

In addition to the requirements imposed in Delaware and Washington, Vermont requires that couples have a civil union license in order for clergy to officiate. Only the three trial liturgies developed by the diocese may be employed.

Those whose unions are blessed must sign a Declaration of Intent very similar in its wording to the declaration signed by opposite-sex couples. The parties state that they,

> desiring to receive the blessing of Holy Union in the Church, do solemnly declare that we hold this partnership to be a lifelong union of persons as described by the Episcopal Church gathered in General Convention. We believe that the union of two partners is intended by God for their mutual joy, for the encouragement and support given one another in daily life and changing circumstances, for the deepening of faith as they experience God's love in their love for one another, and (if it may be) the physical and spiritual nurture of children. Such relationships are nurtured and characterized by fidelity, monogamy, mutual affection and respect, careful, honest communication, and the holy love which enables those in such relationships to see in each other the image of God. And we do engage ourselves, so far as in us lies, to make our utmost effort to establish this relationship and to seek God's help hereto.

The first of the three permissible liturgies is adapted from use of St. Thomas in Washington, D.C., by now familiar to readers of this work. The second is very close to the Prayer Book rite, with the influence of the California and Consultation rites somewhat evident. The third rite is what clergy are wont to refer to as a "Rite III" service, that is, an outline such as the Prayer Book provides for the Eucharist or weddings where special crafting is desired. That outline is included below (p. 144).

The Vermont rites all include vows specifically so called, for life. In each rite a pair of options is given. The vows are the only fixed texts in the Rite III liturgy. This parallels the requirement in the Rite III Prayer Book service, ensuring the communal nature and communal investment in the unions — we all promise the same thing. The second form is in the familiar language of the Prayer Book:

> N., I join my life with yours, from this day forward. In prosperity and in hardship, in health and in sickness, in joy and in sorrow,

I will love and cherish you as long as we both shall live. This I vow before God.

or

In the name of God, I, N., take you, N., to be my partner in life, to have and to hold from this day forward, for better for worse, for richer for poorer, in sickness and in health, to love and to cherish until we are parted by death. This is my solemn vow.

The diocese further commits itself to providing resources for congregations, couples, and clergy. The document includes a bibliography.

The Diocese of Massachusetts has a study under way, but its results are not public at the time of this writing.

Conclusion

As promised, this essay cannot contribute much to the debate over whether or not the church can or should endorse the blessing of same-sex couples. What I hope has become clear is that by and large, the liturgical patterns being suggested are not foreign to what users of the Prayer Book know. Colloquially, with the exception of the crowning ritual suggested by the Consultation, there is nothing here to scare the liturgical horses.

At the same time, it is clear that there is no monolithic liturgical consensus regarding the nature and content of a rite for blessing these unions, and what blessing amounts to.

Finally, whether or not the church endorses the blessing of same-sex vows, an enormous amount of work has gone into these rites, some of it representing new or richer language for expressing the sacramentality of life commitment. It would seem that liturgical revisers working on marriage rites of any kind would want to consult the wealth of material of which this essay has provided only a tiny sample.

The variety of concepts regarding the nature of the union contracted and how far it is desirable or accurate to use the images of marriage for same-sex unions indicates the degree to which work must still be done and underscores the delicate relationship between rite and life. How these rites are formulated will express our thinking and experience. How they are celebrated will shape perceptions and expectations of the relationships the church blesses.

Part Three

LITURGIES

St. Luke in the Fields, New York City

*The Covenanting and Blessing
of the Lifelong Union
of Anne Bursley Bost and Brenda Kay Bost*

Prelude

Entrance Hymn

THE WORD OF GOD

Acclamation

Gloria in Excelsis

The Collect of the Day

Celebrant

Let us pray. O gracious and everliving God, look joyfully upon Anne and Brenda, who come before this assembled community to make a covenant of love, fidelity, and lifelong commitment. Grant them your blessing and assist them with your grace, that, with true fidelity and steadfast love, they may honor and keep the covenant they make, through Jesus Christ, our Savior, who lives and reigns with you in the unity of the Holy Spirit, forever and ever. *Amen.*

The rites in this chapter have been lightly edited for consistency of format so as not to distract the reader from their content.

The First Lesson	Wisdom 8:9–16
Anthem	
The Second Lesson	1 Corinthians 13:1–13
Sequence Hymn	
The Holy Gospel	Matthew 5:1–10
The Homily	

THE COVENANTING AND BLESSING

The celebrant asks the couple

What do you seek?

The couple responds in unison

We ask a blessing from this community on our covenant.

The celebrant asks the couple

Who sponsors you in this commitment?

The people stand and respond in unison

We do in the belief that God has blessed Anne and Brenda by calling them into this covenant with each other.

The celebrant then addresses the people, saying

Will you, brothers and sisters in Christ, give your pledge to honor and uphold Anne and Brenda, to recognize them as a family in this community, to guide and pray for them in times of trouble, to celebrate with them in times of joy, to respect the bonds of their covenant, and to seek to discern the continuing presence of Christ within them?

The people respond

We will.

Each partner of the couple vows

In the name of God and before this congregation, I, *N.*, promise you, *N.*, to honor and cherish you, to share with you in life's joys and triumphs, and to stand with you in times of grief and misfortune. I will be truthful in all things and strive with you to create a home filled with reverence and hospitality. I promise to love you all the days of my life. This is my solemn vow.

The rings are then blessed. The giver places the ring on the finger of the other's hand, saying

I give you this ring as a symbol of my vow to you, my friend, my sister, my partner, my spouse. In the Name of the Father, and of the Son, and of the Holy Spirit. Amen.

The celebrant joins the right hands of the couple. The people say in unison

May the God who has given Anne and Brenda the grace to love one another and to enter into this covenant, give them the strength and power to walk in it all of their days. Amen.

All remain standing as the deacon bids the intercessions.

The Prayers of the People

The intercessor will say or sing

Let us pray for the Church and for the world.
Grant, Almighty God, that all who confess your Name may be united in your truth, live together in your love, and reveal your glory in the world.
Lord, in your mercy
Hear our prayer.

Bless Anne and Brenda in their lifelong covenant. Give them wisdom and devotion in the ordering of their common life, that each may be to the other a strength in need, a counselor in perplexity, a comfort in sorrow, and a companion in joy.
Lord in your mercy
Hear our prayer.

Grant that their wills may be so knit together in your will, and their spirits in your Spirit, that they may grow in love and peace with you and one another all the days of their life.
Lord in your mercy
Hear our prayer.

Give them grace, when they hurt each other, to recognize and acknowledge their fault, and to seek each other's forgiveness and yours.
Lord in your mercy
Hear our prayer.

Make their life together a sign of Christ's love to a sinful and broken world, that unity may overcome estrangement, forgiveness heal guilt, and joy conquer despair.
Lord in your mercy
Hear our prayer.

Give them such fulfillment of their mutual affection that they may reach out in love and concern for others.
Lord in your mercy
Hear our prayer.

Bless all whose lives are closely linked with ours, and grant that we may serve Christ in them, and love one another as he loves us.
Lord, in your mercy
Hear our prayer.

Comfort and heal all those who suffer in body, mind, or spirit; give them courage and hope in their troubles, and bring them the joy of your salvation.
Lord, in your mercy
Hear our prayer.

We commend to your mercy all who have died, that your will for them may be fulfilled; and we pray that we may share with all your saints in your eternal kingdom.

Lord, in your mercy
Hear our prayer.

The Blessing of the Union

The people remain standing.

The couple kneel, and the priest says the following prayer

O God, lover of humankind, in whom all our covenants are established, send your blessing upon your servants Anne and Brenda, that they may so love, honor, and cherish each other in faithfulness and patience, in wisdom and true godliness, that their home may be a haven of blessing and peace; through Jesus Christ, our Lord, who lives and reigns with you and the Holy Spirit, one God, now and forever. *Amen.*

The couple still kneeling, the celebrant adds this blessing

God the Father, God the Son, God the Holy Spirit, bless, preserve, and keep you; the Lord mercifully with his favor look upon you, and fill you with all spiritual benediction and grace; that you may faithfully live together in this life, and in the age to come have life everlasting. *Amen.*

The Peace

THE HOLY COMMUNION

Offertory Anthem

The Great Thanksgiving: Eucharistic Prayer B, Prayer Book, p. 367

Preface of Ascension

The Lord's Prayer

Fraction Anthem: Agnus Dei

Postcommunion Prayer: Prayer Book, p. 365

Blessing

Dismissal

Consultation on Blessing of Same-Sex Unions

Section Two: A Rite for the Celebration of Commitment to a Life Together

INTRODUCTION

This rite is intended for use as a public celebration of commitment to a life together between two persons, at least one of whom is a baptized Christian, and who desire to celebrate their commitment in the context of the Christian community. The rite consists of two parts.

In Part I, the couple declare to their families, friends, and congregations(s) their intention to explore their relationship and to begin a period of discernment, assisted by sponsors and ideally a small group from within the congregation, who help them discern the nature of their relationship and articulate their expectations and fears and the commitments that they are ready to make.

In Part II, the couple celebrate their commitment to each other, responding to the proclamation of God's Word by exchanging vows. The presider leads the assembly in thanking God for God's love and faithfulness, manifested by the couple's commitment, and pronounces God's blessing upon them.

A suitable period of time should transpire between the two parts of the rite. For pastoral reasons, Part II may be celebrated without the first having taken place.

PART I: DECLARATION OF INTENT

This rite initiates a period of preparation leading to Part II. The Declaration of Intention may take place in the context of the Sunday Eucharist in the congregation to which one or both partners belong. Alternatively, it may be celebrated at any time or place.

The Eucharist begins as usual. Before the Song of Praise, the presider may welcome the people in these or similar words

Welcome. Today, N. and N. come before us, to declare their intention to join their lives together and to request our support as they prepare for their commitment. As their friends and family we rejoice with them and give thanks to God for calling them together in love.

We invite you to express your support of N. and N. and their relationship by participating fully throughout the service.

The service continues with the Song of Praise, Collect, and Readings. The readings are those appointed for the given Sunday.

Following the Prayers of the People, the presider invites the couple to stand in full view of the congregation and introduces them.

Declaration of Intent

The presider or the couple may then address the people, explaining their decision to begin preparations for their celebration and announcing its date, if it has been decided. They may ask for the support and prayers of their congregation(s).

The couple addresses the presider

N., we come before you today to share our joy with this congregation and to seek its support and prayers as we journey into our commitment to a life together.

The presider addresses each partner

N., do you freely intend to commit yourself to N. as your partner in life?

Response   I do. Blessed be God who visits me in N.'s love.

The presider addresses the sponsors

N.N. you have been selected to accompany N. and N. as they journey together in commitment, in love, and in faithfulness. As you share their joys, will you help support them in their preparation and help carry their burdens?

Sponsors   We will. Blessed be God who appears to us in their love.

The presider addresses the congregation

As N. and N.'s family in Christ, will you rejoice in their love?

People   We will. Blessed be God who appears to us in their love.

Presider   Will you support them as they grow in love and faithfulness?

People   We will. Blessed be God who appears to us in their love.

Rings or gifts may be exchanged in silence.

Prayer over the Couple

The presider, and if desired the sponsors, may lay hands on the couple. The presider then says

Creator and Healer of all that is,
you make the heavens and the earth by your loving Word
and give yourself to us in love.
Be present now, with N. and N.
as they prepare to give themselves to each other.
By your Word, affirm in them your new creation
and unite them in the bond of peace,
as you promised through Jesus Christ, who said,
"My peace I give you, my own peace I give to you."
for you are the fountain of all peace,
and to you we give praise and thanks, Source, Word, and Spirit,
one God, in glory everlasting.

People   *Amen.*

The liturgy continues with the Peace and the Offertory. The couple may present the offerings of bread and wine.

PART II: THE CELEBRATION OF COMMITMENT TO A LIFE TOGETHER

Part II is designed to take place in the context of the Sunday Eucharist in the congregation to which one or both partners belong. If necessary, for pastoral reasons, the rite may be celebrated at another time.

The Eucharist begins as usual. Before the Song of Praise, the presider welcomes the people in these or similar words

Welcome to the celebration of N. and N.'s commitment to each other as life partners. The Christian community recognizes that the love between two people manifests God's love. Today we celebrate N. and N.'s love as a gift from God to them and to all of us. As they formally commit to their life together, we bless and thank God for this gift to us.

Here follows the Song of Praise.

If the Declaration of Intent did not take place on an earlier occasion, the following declaration may be used.

The presider addresses each partner

N., have you made a free decision and do you have the firm intention to enter into this commitment with N., who stands here before you, having promised yourself to no other?

Response	I have.
Presider	The Lord be with you.
People	And also with you.
Presider	Let us pray.

O God our Maker and Lover of the heavens and the earth, you have taught us to love each other as Christ loved us, to bear each other's burdens, and to share each other's strengths. Look with favor on *N.* and *N.*, whom you have brought together in love. Grant them sincere love, and unfailing strength. Protect them in their life and work and lead them with us and all creation into our reign of justice and peace. We ask this through Jesus Christ our Savior, who lives with you and the Holy Spirit, now and for ever. *Amen.*

The readings are normally those appointed for the given Sunday. For pastoral reasons, one or more of the following readings may be used.

From the Hebrew Bible

> Song of Solomon 2:10–13; 8:6–7 (Many waters cannot quench love)
> 1 Samuel 18:1b, 3; 20:16–17, 42a (Jonathan made a covenant with David...)
> Ruth 1:16–17 (Where you go I will go...)
> Ecclesiastes 4:9–12 (Two are better than one)

From the Psalms

> 67, 85, 111, 127, 133:1–3, 149

From the New Testament

> Romans 12:9–21 (Let love be genuine)
> 1 Corinthians 13:1–13 (If I speak with the tongues of mortals...)
> Colossians 3:12b–16a (Be clothed in sincere compassion)
> 1 John 4:7–12 (Beloved let us love one another)

From the Gospels

> Matthew 7:24–27 (The house built on the rock)
> Luke 6:20–23 (The Beatitudes)
> John 2:1–12a (The marriage at Cana)
> John 15:9–17 (This is my commandment: that you love one another)
> John 17:1, 18–26 (...that they may be one as we are one)

The Vows

The presider invites the couple to stand in full view of the congregation. The couple face each other. Taking the other's hand, each says to the other

N., I give myself to you.

The other responds

N., I take you to have and to hold from this day forward, to love and to cherish, for better or worse, in sickness and in health, as my companion, lover, and friend. This is my solemn vow.

Deacon   People of God, give praise to God.
People   Blessed be God who appears to us in their love.

The Exchange of Rings or Gifts

The presider may say

Praise and thanks to you, O God.
You give yourself to us
in love and faithfulness.
Bless these rings [or gifts]
as enduring signs of
N. and N.'s commitment to each other.
Keep them in the bond of love
through Christ our Savior. *Amen.*

Each person places the ring on the ring-finger of the other's hand, or presents the gift(s), saying

N., I give you this ring (or gift) as a sign of my love and faithfulness. With my body I honor you, and all that I possess I share with you.

Deacon   People of God, give praise to God.
People   Blessed be God who appears to us in their love.

The Prayers of the People

Presider   Seeing how greatly God has loved us, let us lift up before God this couple, this community of faith, and the whole world, saying, Hear our prayer.

The deacon or an appointed layperson bids the people to pray, employing this or some other form

Deacon   I ask your prayers for the earth and all of God's creation: for the rivers and oceans, for the forests and fields, for the mountains and meadows, and for all creatures who live in them. Pray for our planet.

The people pray aloud.

Deacon   O God, source of all life,
People   Hear our prayer.
Deacon   I ask your prayers for the welfare of the world, for peace and respect among nations, for all the leaders of the world, and for all men and women and children everywhere. Pray for the world.

The people pray aloud.

Deacon   O God, source of all life
People   Hear our prayer.
Deacon   I ask your prayers for our country, for those who govern, and for all in authority. Pray for justice in our own land.

The people pray aloud.

Deacon   O God, source of all life,
People   Hear our prayer.
Deacon   I ask your prayers for the concerns of our community, for the people of this [neighborhood, town, city], and for the yearnings of our hearts which we now present before God. Pray for our community.

The people pray aloud.

Deacon	O God, source of all life,
People	Hear our prayer.
Deacon	I ask your prayers for those who suffer; pray for the sick and the poor, the destitute, the unemployed, the lonely, the bereaved, the victims of addiction, and the victims of hatred and intolerance. Pray for those who bear the pain of the world.

The people pray aloud.

Deacon	O God, source of all life,
People	Hear our prayer.
Deacon	I ask your prayers for the Christian community everywhere: for our life and ministry, for our bishop(s), and for all leaders, that we may be the risen Body of Christ in the world. Pray for the Church.

The people pray aloud.

Deacon	O God, source of all life,
People	Hear our prayer.
Deacon	I ask your prayers for N. and N.: for their life together, that they may be filled with God's blessing and grow in love for each other with faithfulness throughout their life together. Pray for N. and N.

The people pray aloud.

Deacon	O God, source of all life,
People	Hear our prayer.
Deacon	I ask your prayers for N. and N.: for the courage to recognize and forgive each other's faults as they bear each other's burdens. Pray for N. and N.

The people pray aloud.

Deacon	O God, source of all life,
People	Hear our prayer.

Deacon   I ask your prayers of gratitude for all those who are bound to us in love: for our families, friends, neighbors, for all who have gone before us in the faith, and for those whose faith is known to God alone. [I ask your prayers for _____ .] Pray for those we love.

The people pray aloud.

Deacon   O God, source of all life,
People   Hear our prayer.

The presider adds this or another concluding Collect

God of all, you make us in your image and likeness and fill us with everlasting life. You taught your disciples to be united by the law of love. Hear the prayers of your people and grant to N. and N. grace to love each other in joy all the days of their lives. We ask this through Jesus Christ in the Holy Spirit, to whom, with you, one God, be praise for ever and ever. *Amen.*

The Blessing

The couple stand. The presider and the sponsors (and, if desired, the congregation) may lay hands on the couple. The couple may stand at the table with right hands joined upon the Gospel book or Bible. The presider may bind their hands together.

Presider

Praise and thanks to you, O God,
Creator and sustainer of the world.
You spoke and the heavens came into being,
the earth and everything that lives.
You looked and found it good.
The world was charged with your glory and mercy.
Praise and thanks to you, O God,
Liberator and Healer of the world.
You have broken down the wall of division,
calling together by the law of love those who were apart.

For this, Christ died, giving birth to a new creation.
Praise and thanks to you, O Lord our God.
You renew the face of the earth.
Pour your Holy Spirit upon N. and N.
Let them love each other openly without fear,
a joyful sign of your new creation in justice, love and peace.

Deacon   People of God, give praise to God.
People   Blessed be God who appears to us in their love.

Presider

The living God bless you.
May you flourish together
and rejoice in your friends.
[May God bless your children.]
May God grant you the goods that endure
and bring you everlasting joy.
And the blessing of the Living God,
The Source, the Word and the Spirit,
be upon you now and forever. *Amen.*

The liturgy continues immediately with the Peace. The couple kiss and the congregation welcomes them by greeting them and each other. During or after the exchange of the Peace, the following anthem (Ps. 85:10, 22) may be sung.

Mercy and truth have met together; *
righteousness and peace have kissed each other.
Truth shall spring up from the earth, *
and righteousness shall look down from heaven.

The service continues with the Eucharist. The couple may present the offerings of bread and wine.

Diocese of New Westminster

The Blessing of Same-Sex Unions
(First Version, November 1, 2000)

THE GATHERING OF THE COMMUNITY

The people stand. The couple stand before the presider, with their sponsors.

Presider   The Grace of our Lord Jesus Christ, and the love of God,
              and the fellowship of the Holy Spirit, be with you all.
People   And also with you.
Presider   Beloved People of God,

We have come together in the presence of God to witness and bless
the covenant of love and fidelity which *N.N.* and *N.N.* have made
with each other. The union of two persons in heart, body, and mind
is intended by God for their mutual joy; for the help and comfort
given one another in prosperity and adversity; and that their love
may be a blessing to all whom they encounter. This solemn covenant is not to be entered into unadvisedly or lightly, but reverently,
deliberately, and with the commitment to seek God's will for their
lives.

THE PROCLAMATION OF THE WORD

*Two or three readings, including a Gospel reading, shall normally be read.
Members of the family and friends of the couple may read.*

A psalm, canticle, hymn, anthem, or period of silence may follow the readings.

A sermon or reflection may follow.

Intent

Presider   N.N. and N.N., what do you seek?

Couple   We come before God, you, and this community; believing that we belong to each other and together we belong to God. We ask for God's blessing and the blessing of the church on our life together.

The presider then asks each partner in turn

Presider   N.N., will you share your love and life with N.N., your wholeness and your brokenness, your joys and your sorrows, your health and your sickness, your riches and your poverty, your success and your failure, and be faithful to *him/her* so long as you both shall live?

Answer   I will.

Support and Blessing of the Community

Presider   Will you, the families, friends, and faith community of N.N. and N.N., promise to honour and uphold them in their life together; to recognize them as a household; to guide and pray for them in times of trouble; to celebrate with them in times of joy; to respect the bounds of their covenant; and to seek to discern the continuing presence of Christ in their lives?

People   We will, with God's help.

Presider   Do you give them your blessing?

People   We do.

Presider

N.N. and N.N. have been duly prepared to enter into this relationship. They have stated their intent, they will exchange solemn vows, and in token of this, they will (each) exchange symbol(s) of their vows. We pray with them that by God's help they may fulfil God's purpose for the whole of their earthly life together.

Let us pray,

O God our Creator, lover of heaven and earth,
you have taught us to love each other
as Christ loved us,
to bear each other's burdens,
and to share each other's strengths.
Look with favour upon N.N. and N.N.,
whom you have brought together in love.
Grant them sincere love and unfailing strength.
Protect them in their life and in their work,
and lead them with us and all creation
into your realm of justice and peace.
We ask this through Jesus Christ our Saviour,
who lives with you and the Holy Spirit,
one God, now and forever.

People   Amen.

Vows

The presider invites the couple to stand in full view of the congregation and face each other. Taking each other's hands, each says to the other in turn

N.N., I give myself (*again*) to you.
I love you, I trust you, I delight in you.
I will bear your burdens,
I will share your joys
and I will go with you
wherever God calls us.
This is my solemn vow.

The presider addresses the couple together

Presider	N.N. and N.N., do you believe God has called you to live together in love?
Couple	We do believe.
Presider	Will you continue to be faithful to each other?
Couple	We will, with God's help.

Presider	Will you, under God, recognize each other's freedom to grow as individuals and allow each other time and space so to do?
Couple	We will, with God's help.
Presider	Will you do all in your power to make your life together a witness to the love of God in the world?
Couple	We will, with God's help.

The Blessing of Rings; or other symbol(s)

The presider receives the rings and addresses the congregation in these or similar words

Presider	Praise and thanks to you, O God of grace. You give yourself to us in love and faithfulness. Bless these rings as enduring signs of *N.N.'s* and *N.N.'s* commitment to each other. Keep them in the bond of love through Christ our Saviour.
People	Amen.

or...

Presider	May God bless these rings already worn down by years of shared work, play, quiet, companionship, and joy. May they be the outward sign of God's indwelling grace in your love.

or...

Presider	Dear friends in Christ, let us ask God to bless these rings, that they may be symbols of the vow and covenant *N.N.* and *N.N.* have made this day.

The community may pray silently. The presider then says

Presider	Blessed are you, God of steadfast love, source of our joy and end of our hope. Bless these rings given and received through Jesus Christ our Lord.
People	Amen.

The couple place the ring on the ring finger of each other's hand and say, in turn

N.N., I give you this ring as a symbol of my vow. With all that I am and all that I have, I honour you in the name of God.

The Prayers of the People

The Prayers of the People may be led by friend(s) or member(s) of a family of the couple, or by the presider or another minister. [Two additional forms are provided.]

Leader	Let us pray. Eternal God, creator and preserver of all life, author of salvation, and giver of grace: Look with favour upon the world you have made, and for which your son Jesus gave his life and especially upon these two persons whose covenant you bless. God, in your love,
People	Hear our prayer.
Leader	Give them wisdom and devotion in the ordering of their common life, that each may be to the other a strength in need, a counselor in perplexity, a comfort in sorrow, and a companion in joy. God, in your love,
People	Hear our prayer.
Leader	Grant that their wills may be so knit together in your will, and their spirits in your Spirit, that they may grow in love and peace with you and one another all the days of their lives. God, in your love,
People	Hear our prayer.
Leader	Make their life together a sign of Christ's love to this broken world, that unity may overcome estrangement, forgiveness heal guilt, and joy conquer despair. God, in your love,
People	Hear our prayer.
Leader	Give them such fulfilment of their mutual affection that they may reach out in love and concern for others. God, in your love,
People	Hear our prayer.

Leader	Grant that we who have witnessed these vows may find our lives strengthened and our loyalties confirmed. God, in your love
People	Hear our prayer.

If the Eucharist is not to be celebrated, the prayers conclude with the Lord's Prayer.

The Blessing of the Union

The people remain standing. The couple stands or kneels before the presider, and the celebrant says the following prayers.

Most gracious God, we give you thanks for your tender love in sending Jesus Christ to come among us, to be born of a human mother, and to make the way of the cross to be the way of life. By the power of your Holy Spirit, pour out your abundant blessing upon N.N. and N.N. Defend them from every enemy. Lead them in all peace. Let their love for each other be a seal upon their hearts, a mantle upon their shoulders, and a crown upon their foreheads. Bless them in their work and their companionship, in their sleeping and in their waking, in their joys and in their sorrows, in their life and in their death. Finally in your mercy, bring them to that table where your saints feast forever in your banquet; through Jesus Christ our Lord, who with you and the Holy Spirit lives and reigns one God, now and forever.

People	Amen.

This additional blessing may be added

Presider	God the Father, God the Son, God the Holy Spirit, (*God; Creator, Redeemer, and Giver of Life*) bless, preserve, and keep you; may God mercifully look with favour upon you, and fill you with all spiritual benediction and grace; that you may faithfully live together in this life, and in the age to come have life everlasting.
People	Amen.

The Peace

Presider   Dear friends in Christ.
            The peace of God be with you.
People   And also with you.

The couple may greet each other and the community shares a sign of peace.

If the Eucharist is not to be celebrated, the service may conclude with: a presentation of the couple, a blessing of the congregation, a dismissal.

THE LITURGY OF THE EUCHARIST

It is appropriate that the couple prepare bread and wine for the Eucharist and that they present the elements to the altar. The Eucharistic Prayer may be taken from the BCP, the BAS, the New Westminster Supplemental Eucharistic texts, or the Supplemental Prayers of the ACC 1998. Form A and B from the New Westminster Supplemental texts allow for substantial particularisation of the text.

The Preparation of the Gifts

Presider   Let us pray.
People   God of the covenant, hear our prayer, and accept all we offer you this day. May the mystery of Christ's unselfish love, which we celebrate in this Eucharist, increase our love for you and for each other, through Christ our Lord. Amen.

Prayer after Communion

Presider   Let us pray.
People   Gracious God, may N.N. and N.N., who are joined together in these holy mysteries, become one in heart and soul. May they live in fidelity and peace and obtain those eternal joys prepared for all who love you; through your Son, Jesus Christ our Lord. Amen.

Presider Glory to God,

People whose power, working in us, can do infinitely more than we can ask or imagine. Glory to God from generation to generation, in the Church and in Christ Jesus, for ever and ever. Amen.

Dismissal

Diocese of New Westminster

The Celebration of a Covenant
(Second Version, May 2003)

GATHERING OF THE COMMUNITY

Greeting

As the community gathers, a hymn, anthem, or canticle may be sung. Instrumental music may also be played.

The presider welcomes the community

May the grace of our Lord Jesus Christ, and the love of God, and the communion of the Holy Spirit be with you all.
And also with you.

After the greeting the presider may continue as follows

Holy and Eternal One, in the quiet night you have called us each by our own name.
In our very heart you have named us beloved.

You surprise us by your grace.
We are the fruit of your boundless love.

On our exodus way you nourish and free us.
You give us companions for our journey.

You set us apart, shaped by our love, yet call us into the midst of your people,
Where we will be your word of blessing.

Here follows one of the following Collects

Let us pray,

Blessed are you, O Holy One, for you are pleased to dwell among us and to fill our lives with your presence. May N. and N. who seek your blessing upon their covenant be filled with your love. May their life together be to us a sign of your promised reign of justice and peace. We ask this in the name of Jesus Christ our Lord who with you and the Holy Spirit lives and reigns, one God, now and for ever. *Amen.*

Or

Searching and saving God, whose unfailing love alone can satisfy our longing, in your mercy you befriend those who wander in loneliness and shame, those oppressed because of difference, those who do not know the value of their unique and sacred gift. By your Holy Spirit you awaken in them the dignity of human being and the responsibility of embodied love, as perfected by Jesus Christ, who loved and gave himself for us, showing us the way to intimacy with you and with one another. We offer praise and thanks to you, our Creator, Redeemer, and Life-giver, for your love endures for ever. *Amen.*

Or

Blessed are you, loving God, for you awaken our desire for companionship and our hope for community with you and with one another. In your mercy you call us out of solitary darkness and redeem us to love you with our whole heart, soul, mind, and strength. Renew in us a sense of true belonging and call us to love our neighbour as ourselves. We pray that the covenant of faithfulness and love we celebrate today will reflect your unending faithfulness and great love for the world. May N. and N. so love one another that they may be a blessing to you and all whom they encounter. We ask these things in thanksgiving and praise to you, our Creator, Redeemer, and Sustainer, one God now and for ever. *Amen.*

PROCLAMATION OF
THE WORD OF GOD

The Readings

Two or three readings, including a Gospel reading, shall normally be read. If the Holy Communion is celebrated, then a Gospel reading must be included. Members of the family and friends of the couple may read the lessons. It is appropriate to respond to a reading with a psalm, canticle, hymn, anthem, instrumental music, or silence.

The following readings are appropriate for the celebration of a covenant. Other readings may be chosen in consultation with the presider.

Ruth 1:16–18; Song of Solomon 2:1–13; Song of Solomon 3:1–4; Song of Solomon 8:6–7; Ecclesiastes 4:9–12;

Psalm 100:1–5; Psalm 107:1–9; Psalm 108:1–5; Psalm 111; Psalm 112; Psalm 126:1–3; Psalm 133; Psalm 139:1–18, 23–24; Psalm 145; Psalm 146;

Romans 12:9–21; 1 Corinthians 13:1–13; 2 Corinthians 5:16–20; Galatians 5:13–14, 22–26; Ephesians 4:25–27, 29–32; Philippians 2:1–4; Colossians 3:12–17; 1 John 3:18–24; 1 John 4:7–21;

Matthew 5:1–16; Luke 6:32–38; John 15:9–17; John 17:1, 18–26.

At the conclusion of readings from the Hebrew Bible and the New Testament writings other than the Gospels, the reader says

Hear what the Spirit is saying to the Church.
Thanks be to God.

All stand for the Gospel. The reader says

The Lord be with you.
And also with you.

The Holy Gospel of our Lord Jesus Christ according to . . .
Glory to you, Lord Jesus Christ.

At the conclusion of the Gospel, the reader says
The Gospel of Christ.
Praise to you, Lord Jesus Christ.

The Sermon

THE COVENANT

The presider invites the couple to stand in the full view of the gathered community and addresses the couple in these or similar words

A covenant is an ancient form of promise, a public declaration of commitment that binds people in an enduring relationship. The Bible tells the story of God's covenant with human beings. God's covenant with Israel was the basis of the people's liberation from slavery and exile. God's covenant with the followers of Jesus brings us into a new community where there is no male nor female, Jew nor Greek, slave nor free, but one people united in Christ. All our covenants with family and friends are signs of God's faithfulness and love. They are living expressions of God's promises to us and sources of hope to others. Today we gather to witness and to bless the public commitment of N. and N. to such a covenant.

The presider then addresses the couple as follows

N. and N., do you believe God has called you into a lifelong covenant of love and fidelity?

Couple   We do believe.

Will you live together in love?

Couple   We will, with God's help.

Will you be faithful to one another?

Couple   We will, with God's help.

Will you support one another in love so that you may both grow into maturity of faith in Jesus Christ?

Couple   We will, with God's help.

Will you do all in your power to make your life together a witness to the love of God in the world?

Couple   We will, with God's help.

The presider invites the couple to stand in full view of the congregation and to face each other. Taking each other by the hand(s), each says to the other in turn

N., I give myself to you. I love you, trust you, and delight in you. I will share your burdens and your joys. I will go with you wherever God calls us. This is my solemn promise.

The Blessing of the Covenant

The presider then addresses the community as follows

You, friends and members of the families of N. and N., are witnesses to this covenant. Will you support N. and N. in the promises they have made?
We will.

Will you celebrate the goodness of God's grace evident in their lives?
We will.

Will you stand by them, encourage, guide, and pray for them in times of trouble and distress?
We will.

Do you give them your blessing?
We do.

The presider then says one of the following blessings

Let us pray.
We give thanks and praise to you, O gracious God, for your unfailing love and wonderful deeds among us: for the splendour of creation, the beauty of this world, the mystery of our lives, and the surprises of human love. We give you thanks and praise for N. and N., because you create in them the desire for intimacy and companionship, calling them out of isolation and exile, strengthening them against prejudice and fear, and embracing them in a

family of friends and loved ones. Pour out your abundant blessing upon N. and N. May they grow in love for one another and for all your creation. Lead them into accomplishments that satisfy and delight. Grant that in the years ahead they may be faithful to the promises they make this day, and that in the strength of the Holy Spirit they may grow together in the love, joy, and peace of our Saviour Jesus Christ.

Blessed are you, O gracious God, source of all love, now and for ever. Amen.

The Exchange of the Peace

The peace of the Lord be always with you.
(*or* The peace of Christ be always with you.)
And also with you.

The couple greet each other and then greet their families and friends. If there is no celebration of the Holy Communion, then the liturgy continues with the Lord's Prayer and the Commissioning of the Community.

THE HOLY COMMUNION

The Prayer over the Gifts

During the preparation of the bread and wine, a hymn, canticle, or psalm may be sung or instrumental music played. The following prayer may be used

Faithful God, with these gifts you offer us communion in your Servant, Jesus Christ. May we who celebrate this sacrament be filled with the same self-offering love made manifest in him. This we ask in Christ's name. Amen.

[The celebration of the Eucharist.]

THE COMMISSIONING OF THE COMMUNITY

A Litany of Blessing

After communion has been distributed, the presider, a friend, or a member of the family leads the community in the following litany of blessing. Additional petitions may be included if so desired.

Dear friends, N. and N. have been drawn by God into a covenant of mind and body, heart and will. We have celebrated this covenant and pray that the life they share will reflect the love of God for the whole world. Let us join in prayer asking God's blessing upon us as we go forth with N. and N. to proclaim with our lives the reconciling and renewing love of God made known in Jesus Christ.

Abundant God, Lover of all creation, pour out your blessing on us and the covenant we have celebrated.
May we be blessed by you for ever.

In our solitude and our companionship,
May we be blessed by you for ever.

In our acts of tenderness and intimacy,
May we be blessed by you for ever.

In our delight at knowing and being known,
May we be blessed by you for ever.

In our acts of self-sacrifice to build up one another,
May we be blessed by you for ever.

In our being comfort to each other,
May we be blessed by you for ever.

In our passion for justice,
May we be blessed by you for ever.

In our generosity and tenacity,
May we be blessed by you for ever.

In all our fruitfulness,
May we be blessed by you for ever.

The Dismissal

A hymn or anthem may be sung before the dismissal or instrumental music played. The deacon, or other leader, dismisses the people.

Glory to God,
whose power working in us can do infinitely more than we can ask or imagine. Glory to God from generation to generation in the church and in Christ Jesus, for ever and ever. Amen.

Go in peace to love and serve the Lord.
Thanks be to God.

Liturgy Five

The Making of Brothers

[This rite was constructed using some contemporary material, but much was taken from texts that John Boswell saw as "unions." The rite contains no vows and is not a Eucharist, but a giving of rings has been inserted. It was used in a Lutheran church in 2004.]

In the name of the Father and of the Son, and of the Holy Spirit. *Amen.*

In peace we call upon the Lord.
For heavenly peace we call upon you, O Lord.

For the peace of the world
And for this holy place.

That your servants N. and N. may be sanctified with your spiritual direction;
We call upon you, Lord.

That their love may abide all the days of their lives;
We call upon you, Lord.

That they be given all things needed for the enjoyment of life
And be granted faithfulness and sincere love.

Have mercy on us, O God.
Lord, have mercy.

Let us pray. Forasmuch as you, kind Lord and lover of good, are merciful and loving and have established humankind after your image and likeness; bless your servants N. and N., joined together by the bond of the Spirit, granting them peace and love and one-ness of mind. Cleanse their hearts and support their love for one another, through Jesus Christ our Lord. *Amen.*

Lessons: 1 John 4:7–12; John 17:18–26

Sermon

Hymn

Presider

Splendid to us and much desired is the sweet smell of love, estab-lished in the time of the patriarchs, guided by the voices of the prophets, and sanctified by the preaching of the apostles. Of all the beautiful things of the earth, love is the most excellent.

It was love that gathered the holy apostles through love into the haven of the Church. It was love that taught the holy martyrs the patience to bear their sufferings. It was love that allowed the prophets to fulfill their service. Love was the forerunner of the Sav-ior; and it was love offered as a sacrifice that reconciled the world to God.

Let us pray. Grant, O God, to your servants *N.* and *N.*, the love and peace of your holy apostles, which you have bestowed saying, "My peace I give you and I leave you my peace." Turn your holy ear to the prayers we raise, for you are the provider of all good things and the savior of our souls. To you is endless glory, Father, Son and Holy Spirit. *Amen.*

Those for whom we pray place their right hands on the open scriptures.

Presider

O Lord, who grants to us our salvation and has called us to love one another and forgive each other our failings, bless these your servants who love each other with a love of the spirit and have come into this church to be blessed. Grant them fidelity and sincere love. And as you kept your disciples and apostles in your peace and love, grant to N. and N. all they need as they live in your presence. *Amen.*

Rings are brought forth and blessed.

Presider

Creator and preserver of humankind, giver of spiritual grace, who grants salvation; send your blessing upon these rings, forever and ever. Amen.

Each gives a ring to the other, saying

Receive this ring as a witness to my faithfulness and love.

Presider

Almighty God, hear our prayers and kindly assist us with your grace, so that those who are joined together may be preserved by your aid.

The Peace is shared. Then the following prayers are said

Presider

Let us pray. O Lord our God, the designer of love and author of peace, who gives the gift of unity and has given us one another, send now your grace and lovingkindness upon your servants who have come before you this day. Sanctify and fill them with your mercies, and gladden them with your presence. Lord in your mercy, *Hear our prayer.*

Heavenly Father, you are the author of love, the master of peace, and the savior of all. Grant to us your love and guide us to receive one another with love and serve one another in love. Lord in your mercy,
Hear our prayer.

Lead us in your truth;
And help us to serve you.

Our Father...

The Blessing

Holy God, you are glorified in the fellowship of the saints. Bless your servants *N.* and *N.* and grant them knowledge of your Holy Spirit. Guide them in holy fear and grant them joy, that they may become united in spirit; for you bless and sanctify those who trust in you.

The God of Abraham, the God of Isaac, and the God of Jacob be with you; and may God who unites us in peace, pour out his blessing upon you. *Amen.*

Diocese of Washington, D.C.

The Celebration and Blessing
of a Covenant Relationship

A hymn or anthem may be sung as the liturgical ministers enter, either here or after the opening acclamation, in place of the opening dialogue.

The following acclamation, or another acclamation from the Book of Common Prayer or Enriching Our Worship, *begins the rite.*

Presider	Blessed be the One, Holy, and Living God:
People	Glory to God for ever and ever.

The following dialogue may be added

Presider	Beloved, let us love one another,
People	For love is of God.
Presider	Whoever does not love does not know God;
People	For God is love.
Presider	Since God loved us so much;
People	We ought also to love one another.

The Collect of the Day

Presider	God be with you.
or	The Lord be with you.
People	And also with you.
Presider	Let us pray.

Holy and loving God, in our baptism you call us into relationship with you and the whole creation: We thank you for giving us signs of your steadfast love in the covenant of fidelity two people make with one another, and we pray that, in your mercy, you will give your blessing to N. and N. who come before you, and strengthen them day by day with the love of your Holy Spirit that they may be a blessing to one another and to the world; through Jesus Christ our Savior, who lives and reigns with you and the Holy Spirit, one God, for ever and ever. *Amen.*

The Word of God

Then at least two of the following passages from Holy Scripture are read, the final reading being chosen from the Gospel passages. Between the readings a Psalm, hymn, or anthem may be sung or said.

1 Samuel 18:1b, 3; 20:16–17, 42a. or 1 Samuel 18:1–4; Ruth 1:16–17; Ecclesiastes 4:9–12 (New English Bible preferred); Song of Solomon 2:10–13; 8:6–7; Micah 4:1–3, 6–8; Zephaniah 3:14–20; Ecclesiasticus (Sirach) 17:1–3, 6–13

Psalms: 65, 67, 85:7–13, 11, 127, 133, 149, 8, 148

Romans 12:9–21; 1 Corinthians 12:31–13:13; 2 Corinthians 5:17–20; Galatians 5:13–14, 22–26; Philippians 2:1–4; Ephesians 3:14–19; Ephesians 4:25–32; Colossians 3:12b–16a; 1 John 4:7–16, 21; 1 John 3:18–24

Matthew 7:21, 24–27; Matthew 5:1–16; Mark 12:28–34; Luke 6:20–23; Luke 6:32–38; Luke 10:21–24; John 2:1–11; John 15:9–17; John 17:1, 18–26

At the end of the readings is said

The Word of the Lord.

or

Hear what the Spirit is saying to God's people [to the Churches].

People   Thanks be to God.

When the Gospel is read, all stand, and the reading is introduced by the deacon or a priest, saying

The Holy Gospel of Our Savior Jesus Christ according to N.

People   Glory to you, O Christ.

or   Glory to you, Lord Christ.

After the Gospel, the reader says

The Gospel of Christ.

or

The Gospel of the Lord.

People	Praise to you, O Christ.
or	Praise to you, Lord Christ.

The Sermon

The Prayers of the People

It is recommended that either of these forms of the Prayers of the People be used, or any of the forms found in the Book of Common Prayer, or any conforming to the outline for the Prayers of the People found in the Holy Eucharist.

Form I

Leader

Dear Friends, N. and N. have been called by God into a covenant of grace and mutual care. Let us join in prayer, asking God's blessing upon us as we proclaim with our lives the love of God revealed in Christ Jesus.

Abundant God, Lover of all creation, pour out your blessing upon us and upon the covenant we celebrate.
Be among us, Spirit of God.

In solitude and companionship,
Be among us, Spirit of God.

In tenderness and intimacy,
Be among us, Spirit of God.

In knowing and in being known,
Be among us, Spirit of God.

In self-sacrifice and self-offering,
Be among us, Spirit of God.

In comfort and consolation,
Be among us, Spirit of God.

In doing justice and making peace,
Be among us, Spirit of God.

In generosity and hospitality,
Be among us, Spirit of God.

In all our fruitfulness,
Be among us, Spirit of God.

Presider

Gracious and everliving God, look joyfully upon N. and N., and upon this assembled community: Grant us your blessing and assist us with your grace, that with true fidelity and steadfast love we may honor and keep the covenants we make with you and one another; through Jesus Christ our Savior. *Amen.*

Form II

Leader

Let us remember before God N. and N., this community of faith and the whole world, saying, "Receive our prayer."

I ask your prayers for N. and N., that they may be filled with God's blessing and grow in love and faithfulness throughout their life together. O God, source of all life,
Receive our prayer.

May N. and N. have the courage to acknowledge and forgive each other's faults. May their life together be a sign of God's mercy. O God, source of all life,
Receive our prayer.

I ask your prayers for God's creation. May we have the wisdom and will to honor and protect all God's creatures. O God, source of all life,
Receive our prayer.

I ask your prayers for our nation and the world and for all in authority. May justice and wisdom, peace and respect flourish among men and women everywhere. O God, source of all life,
Receive our prayer.

I ask your prayers for this community, for the people of this [neighborhood, town, city] and for the welfare of all. O God, source of all life,
Receive our prayer.

I ask your prayers for those who suffer any need or trouble. We pray for the sick and the poor, the unemployed, the imprisoned, the lonely and the bereaved, those who suffer from addictions, those who perpetrate hatred and intolerance and for their victims. O God, source of all life,
Receive our prayer.

I ask your prayers for Christ's Church throughout the world. For our bishop(s) N. and N., and for all Christians everywhere in their life and ministry.

May we be the living presence of Christ in the world. O God, source of all life,
Receive our prayer.

I ask your prayers of gratitude for all those who have gone before us in faith. [We remember and celebrate especially, N.] O God, source of all life,
Receive our prayer.

Presider

O God, Ruler of all, you make us in your image and likeness and bestow upon us life and blessing. You command your followers to be united by the new commandment of love. Receive the prayers of your people and grant to N. and N. grace to love each other all the days of their lives; for you are a compassionate God and a lover of all creatures, and we glorify you now and forever. *Amen.*

A hymn or anthem may be sung.

The Making of the Covenant

The presider invites the couple and their sponsors to stand in view of all and addresses them and the congregation with these words

Today we gather to witness and to bless the public commitment of N. and N. to a lifelong covenant of fidelity and mutuality. A covenant is an ancient form of promise, a public declaration of commitment that binds people in an enduring relationship. The Bible is the story of God's covenant with humankind, a covenant that, since the days of Noah, God has declared shall not be broken. Each one of us enters such a covenant with God in our Baptism, a covenant which is sealed eternally by the power of the Holy Spirit. This covenant binds us not only to God but to one another in a new community we call the Church, a community in which God shows no partiality.

Each one of us is called to live out the Covenant of Baptism in our daily life and work. For some this includes a special relationship of fidelity and mutuality with another person that becomes a sign of God's steadfast love. These relationships are gifts given by God that the whole world might be blessed through them.

The presider then addresses the sponsors directly

Do you who present this couple believe they are called to live in such a covenant?

Sponsors	We do. We believe their life together to be a blessing from God for themselves and for the world.
Presider	Will you [continue to] support them as companions on their journey?
Sponsors	We will, with God's help.

The presider then says to the congregation

Will you who have witnessed these vows support N. and N. in their covenant, standing by them in encouragement and prayer in times of joy and in times of sorrow?

People   We will.

The presider then addresses the couple

N. and N., do you enter freely into this relationship, and do you believe it to be the relationship to which God has called you?

Couple   We do.

Taking each other by the hand(s), each says to the other in turn

N., I make this covenant with you before God and the Church that I will love you in all the circumstances of our lives. With God's help, I will be faithful to you as long as we both shall live, in mutuality of body and spirit, as a companion in faith, hope, and love for the glory of God and the life of the world.

The Blessing of the Rings or Other Symbols

The presider may ask God's blessing on rings or other symbols of the covenant the couple have made as follows. If the rings have been previously given, the couple may extend their hands toward the presider.

Bless, O God, *these rings* as enduring signs of the covenant N. and N. have made, and keep them in the bond of love, through Christ our Savior. *Amen.*

The giver presents the ring or other symbols with these words. This action may be omitted if rings or other symbols have been previously given.

N., I give you *this ring* as a symbol of the covenant we have made with God and with one another. Amen.

The Blessing of the Covenant

Presider	God be with you.
or	The Lord be with you.
People	And also with you.

Presider	Let us give thanks to the Lord our God.
People	It is right to give God thanks and praise.

It is right to give you thanks, most gracious God, and to praise you for the unfailing love and care and for the great joy and comfort bestowed upon us in the gift of human love. We give you praise and thanks for N. and N., and the covenant of love and faithfulness they have made. Pour out the abundance of your grace upon them. Keep them in your steadfast love; protect them from all danger; fill them with your wisdom and peace; lead them in holy service to each other and the world; and, finally, bring them to that table where all your saints feast for ever.

God the Father, God the Son, and God the Holy Spirit
or
God the Source of Life, God the Word of Love and God the Spirit of Truth

... bless, preserve, and keep you; God mercifully look upon you with favor and fill you with all blessing and grace; that you may faithfully live together in this life and be a light to the world until you come into the age of life everlasting. *Amen.*

The Peace

Presider	The peace of Christ be always with you.
People	And also with you.

The Holy Communion

If for special reason the Holy Communion is not to follow, the service concludes with the Peace, the Lord's Prayer being first said together by the people following the Blessing of the Couple.

Otherwise, the liturgy continues with the Offertory. Any of the Great Thanksgivings from the Book of Common Prayer or Enriching Our Worship may be used. If a Proper Preface is required, it is that of Baptism or of the Season.

In place of the usual Postcommunion Prayer, one of the following may be used.

Gracious God, we thank you for the love made known to us in the Body and Blood of your Son, our Savior Jesus Christ. May this sacrament be to us a reminder of the love through which we are called; may it continue to sustain us on the journey and strengthen us in ministry; in the Name of Jesus Christ our Lord. Amen.

or

Gracious God, we thank you for the gift you have given us in the Body and Blood of your Son, our Savior Jesus Christ: for love and companionship; forgiveness and reconciliation; mercy and joy. Grant that N. and N., having professed their love and commitment one to the other, may grow together, secure in your love, nurtured by your church and sustained by your sacrament; in the Name of Jesus Christ. Amen.

Diocese of Vermont: "Rite III"

An Order for Holy Union Provided for Trial Use in the Diocese of Vermont on July 1, 2004

If it is desired to celebrate a holy union otherwise than as set forth in "A Rite for the Celebration and Blessing of a Holy Union," forms 1 and 2, this Order is used. Normally, the presider is a priest or bishop. Where permitted by civil law, and when no priest or bishop is available, a deacon may function as presider but does not pronounce a blessing. The laws of the State of Vermont and the "Policy for Holy Matrimony and Holy Union" of the Diocese of Vermont having been complied with, the couple, together with their witnesses, families, and friends, assemble in the church or in some other convenient place.

1. The understanding of the Church concerning Holy Union, as it is declared by Resolution C051sa ("on the subject of blessing same-gender relationships") of the 2003 General Convention of the Episcopal Church and the "Policy for Holy Matrimony and Holy Union" of the Diocese of Vermont, which includes the "Declaration of Intention for Holy Union," is briefly stated.

2. The intention of each partner to enter the state of holy union, and their free consent, is publicly ascertained.

3. One or more Readings, one of which is always from Holy Scripture, may precede the exchange of vows. If there is to be a Communion, a Reading from the Gospel is always included.

4. The vows of each partner are exchanged, using one of the following forms:

   N., I join my life with yours, from this day forward. In prosperity and in hardship, in health and in sickness, in joy and in sorrow, I will love and cherish you as long as we both shall live. This I vow before God.

or

In the name of God, I, N., take you, N., to be my partner in life, to have and to hold from this day forward, for better for worse, for richer for poorer, in sickness and in health, to love and to cherish until we are parted by death. This is my solemn vow.

5. The presider declares the union of the couple as life partners, in the Name of the Father, and of the Son, and of the Holy Spirit.

6. Prayers are offered for the couple, for their life together, for the Christian community, and for the world.

7. A priest or bishop pronounces a solemn blessing upon the couple.

8. If there is no Communion, the service concludes with the Peace, the partners first greeting each other. The Peace may be exchanged throughout the assembly.

9. If there is to be a Communion, the service continues with the Peace and the Offertory. The Holy Eucharist may be celebrated either according to Rite One or Rite Two in the Prayer Book or according to the rites in *Enriching Our Worship,* or according to the Order on page 401 of the Prayer Book. The Celebration and Blessing of a Holy Union may be used with any authorized liturgy for the Holy Eucharist. This service then replaces the Ministry of the Word, and the Eucharist begins with the Offertory.

Part Four

HEARING TEST: SERMONS

As a way to test whether I am hearing gay and lesbian Episcopalians correctly, I have placed at the very end of this book two sermons I preached in the summer of 2004 at liturgies where these concerns were paramount. I would be interested to know from gay and lesbian readers whether I have accurately heard their witness (bishop@diobeth.org).

Sermon at "All Together Now," a GLBT and Allies Ecumenical Liturgy

St. John's Lutheran Church, Allentown, Pa., June 12, 2004

Twenty-six years ago my doctoral supervisor told me with some consternation that I have an extraordinary talent for delineating the obvious. With a curse like that on one's head, the only thing to do with it is to go metaphorical and make lemonade.

So let me in fact celebrate what is obvious, if only for a moment before returning to preacherly obscurity. What is obvious on this occasion and for this audience is that the extreme religious right is exactly 50 percent correct. They are certainly correct in their constant insistence that if gay, lesbian, bisexual, and transgendered people meet Jesus Christ, that encounter will change them.

The other 50 percent of this, what they don't understand, is the nature of that change. When you listen to their stories you learn that for those brothers and sisters to meet Jesus Christ does change them all right — but the change is from fearful, guilt-ridden, self-loathing people to men and women who know themselves to be children of God, created for a purpose, and intended by God to be responsible stewards of their sexuality just as they are to be responsible stewards of every other aspect of their person — they claim and live out God's rich blessing on their persons and most sacred relationships.

This is why is it is not an issue of some department of sexual ethics, but an issue of the Gospel itself, that all Christians should now speak loudly that which some have come so slowly, reluctantly, and perhaps fearfully to understand: the Bible is entirely accurate when it says that God is in the business of breaking down the dividing wall of hostility that human beings erect against each other when they detect difference. To miss that is to miss the good news and make God no more than the captive of the human status quo. It is the conservatives, not the progressives, after all, who want to make God a captive of the culture.

We are all here today because we know that, but it is good to say it clearly because it is sadly true that much of world Christianity is still run by people who are in terror of their own sexuality or of sexuality in general, and out of that terror create new generations of young men and women who believe that God despises them as abominations, as spiritually and morally ugly. There are at this moment people importing that antiquated and destructive pseudo-religion into the highest levels of our public life.

Consequently it is an urgent issue of the Gospel to tell these young men and women that they are not ugly but beautiful and that life in abundance is for them without qualification or compromise.

Enough of the obvious. It was my need that you hear a bishop of the church that yesterday buried Ronald Reagan say that, in public, in a conservative corner of a conservative state. But the scriptures just read to us demand a little more than what is obvious, and shape how we live out these truths that have become obvious to a few, truths that are dawning on thousands of people every day about themselves or about their children or neighbors.

Three verses from Romans 12 captivate me as we spend our time together.

Romans 12:12–14: Rejoice in hope, be patient in suffering, persevere in prayer. Contribute to the needs of the saints; extend hospitality to strangers. Bless those who persecute you; bless and do not curse them.

Rejoice, Be patient, Persevere, and so on: these verbs are very active and demanding verbs, and chart a pattern of transformation for those who have come to gospel realizations about themselves and know they have something to share with the world. These verses are realistic about the fact that standing for truth that others do not want to hear is expensive, but they are much more: these verses are pathways to gorgeous and luxuriant growth.

Paul says, "Rejoice in hope." Nobody since Simeon and Anna held the baby Jesus in the temple has as much cause for hope as we do today. Institutions, secular and religious, that have been enemies to racial minorities, to women, and to sexual minorities are changing as God's children have bravely acted on their dignity and demanded to be heard. The transformation of our species that was unleashed in the resurrection of Christ continues to break down walls and raise up those who were crushed. Those who may have to take some slight heat for this from time to time in our official capacities and those who in their personal lives bear the burden of oppression on a daily basis do very well to be in gatherings like this one and many others in June — to rejoice. Rejoice in the sheer joy of being who one is, rejoice in knowing what one knows, and rejoice that we continue to see in every level of society a tide that is turning. Rabbi Friedman, the great student of process in religious organizations, observed that when 25 percent of a group gets behind a new idea, the battle is essentially won. We are way past that, thanks to those brave people, religious or not, in whom the Spirit has moved to insist on their place in the front of life's bus. We are already living in the dawn of a new day, and the person or institution has not yet been born that can reverse a sunrise. Rejoicing in that hope makes other things bearable.

The worst thing we could do with the concluding verse, "bless those who persecute you, bless and do not curse," would be to make it a charter for mealy-mouthed co-dependent obsequiousness. There is a special Christian passive aggression, isn't there, in insulting someone by piously saying, "I'll pray for you." The community of the rainbow, because it is formed by the truth of human dignity, is called to be not that kind of religious sham, but called to be an honest-to-God blessing.

And so it is a blessing, to me and to others. I have learned this from many of the kind yet clear GLBT witnesses in my own church, a church that is suffering a bit right now as it is being reborn. (But birth-pangs are by definition worth it.) From these clear, committed, and faithful people I have learned that it is possible to be uncompromising and yet gentle; it is possible to walk in one's own integrity without destroying that of others. It is possible to offer hospitality to those who would never offer it to you.

From the wider GLBT community I have learned that the blessing you bring the world is much more concrete; it has its own character and idiom. I don't know why people are surprised that the wisdom born of GLBT suffering and joy should be different from conventional wisdom, but people often are. It should not be a surprise. When the majority of Christians began to listen to the unique voices of African American theology they found what was different from the mainstream, and were enriched by it. Those of our churches who have ordained women as priests and pastors have found that, no, they aren't just like the men who go around in collars, but have what is different and enriching to add to the profession of ministry. So it should be no surprise that people are waking up to the fact that gay and lesbian Christians are not just Christians who, in those time-honored words, "happen to be" the way they are sexually. The voices that are being heard in our churches are voices representing unique gifts and graces, unique pain and hope, unique insights into the human struggle.

It was once a great contribution to insist that "we are queer and we are here." There still is a blessing to all concerned in acknowledging who was, is, and always will be here in Christ's family. But the blessing being brought to the churches and the community today is even larger than that. A treasury of examples is displayed in David Nimmons's very helpful book, *The Soul*

Beneath the Skin.[1] Just looking at the male side, Nimmons studies gay men and looks at the contributions their community brings to the larger society. Among his observations is the fact that his subjects demonstrated much higher rates of altruism, caring for others who cannot repay; they teach us new things about friendship between men, and that eternally difficult question, how men can actually be friends with women — a revolution of no small proportion, that one. They are leading us to new questions about the nature of sexual intimacy and relationship in general.

My co-religionist Malcolm Boyd has affirmed that lesbian and gay people have a vocation of involvement in the world, and even speaks of this commitment as "a kind of perpetual Peace Corps. We are meant," he adds, "for something beyond our own . . . concerns." Embrace that. There is a delicious irony in the fact that people who are sitting on the fence trying to decide whether they can "tolerate" you do not know how much you will enrich them, to what degree you will bless them, as St. Paul says, once they have the sense to receive that blessing.

I am grateful, moved, and inspired by how many men and women in the Christian churches are determined to be that blessing. From their witness each of us can be for the world that for which Christ has set us free in the first place.

So, back to the obvious, the point of all this has been to say that there are indeed some of us in the often obtuse Establishment who value what this day celebrates, to say that this is God's gospel work we are doing, and to encourage each person here to rejoice in the unique gifts their experience has given them and to share those gifts for the life of the world. Thank you for letting me be with you today.

---

1. David Nimmons, *The Soul Beneath the Skin: The Unseen Hearts and Habits of Gay Men* (New York: St. Martin's Press, 2002).

Sermon at the Reception of the Priestly Orders of Fr. Peter Francis Pearson

Cathedral of the Nativity, Bethlehem, Pa.
July 10, 2004 (propers for Benedict of Nursia)

Fr. Pearson came to the Episcopal Church because of what he con-
sidered the courage and forthrightness of the General Convention
actions of 2003. He is a well-known creator of religious icons and
teaches in the field as well.

On behalf of Fr. Peter, and for myself, I want to thank all of you for coming out in such numbers to support him at this moment of transition and celebration, and also to thank the generous people of Nativity for making this all work in the middle of construction. Let me also underscore at the very beginning that all persons who have been baptized into Jesus Christ are most welcome to receive and are in fact invited to share Christ's body and blood at this Eucharist.

It is hard to say whether I know less about the writings of Benedict or about the mysteries of icon writing, although I admire both. However, I do know a little about Jesus of Nazareth, and know that the words of the Gospel we have just heard offer us something to consider and particularly enrich this moment for Fr. Peter.

In the Gospel for this feast of Benedict, Jesus speaks of the essential dispossession that must take place in each of us if we are to claim to be his followers, and Jesus tops even that by speaking of the crucifixion that we must embrace at the same time. Luke has Jesus say these words to his fans of the moment, the religious groupies who were on the road with him because it was something like first-century cool to be with the rabbi du jour. The Master accordingly draws a clear line: he wants disciples, not fans; he wants followers, not admirers. So he says, "You cannot follow me if you love anything or anyone more; you cannot follow me if you aren't prepared to go to your excruciating moment time and again." Oddly enough, of course, we cannot follow Jesus if we don't think that this dispossession and this crucifixion are nonetheless very small compared to the experience of God's love. Yes, our dispossession and crucifixion are very small because it is also true that Jesus continues to love and call us even on those days when we cling to what we think are possessions, when we love something or someone more than Jesus, days when we flee crucifixion with all our strength. But the challenge and the call are there nonetheless, so let me say two words about the costs and benefits involved in what we do today.

The first is, I don't want you who know him to worry that in becoming a priest in the Episcopal Church Peter is being lost in a sea of ambiguity or mannered mush, doomed to being a parody of some minor character on *Masterpiece Theatre*, a tweedy twit lost in a fifth-century liturgical theme park while the world disintegrates. Contrary to some appearances, the Episcopal Church is not "Catholic Lite," a kind of unreasonable facsimile of real religion replacing devotion to the Theotokos with reverence for the pipe organs of E. M. Skinner — you *can* have both. In our best moments we understand ourselves, with all our struggles and awkwardnesses, to have something distinct to contribute to the life of the entire Christian family *without seeking to dominate it*. I am well aware that to some Christians we appear amateurish and to others we can seem obsessed with ritual irrelevancies. I see that somewhat differently, of course, or I would be practicing law.

The reality is that while we focus strongly on maintaining historic order and creedal orthodoxy, we see ourselves risking a dynamic and open relationship with the Holy Spirit. We avoid as far as we can replacing that supremely risky relationship with the controlling safety of a tightly wrapped religious system where some are counted in and others are excluded by the powerful. It sounds good, and it is good, but count the cost of that kind of church life. Fr. Peter accepts a huge challenge in becoming part of this communion, a family in which we do most of our learning communally, and often experientially, a family where disagreement is standard, a family now at tremendous odds with itself as it attempts to respond to the Spirit's leading. For example, we all know the Bible has God saying in the past, "Behold, I do a new thing," and that was fine, in its day. It is not always as easy to be confronted with God doing a new thing in the present, especially in what we tend to think of as a present that we own and control. In short, to become an Episcopalian is to enter a conversation that sometimes challenges, sometimes delights, sometimes transforms, and sometimes drains. So I want to assure you that Fr. Peter is not escaping serious religion, but that he is being plunged into a somewhat different end of Christ's one great baptismal pool. No matter what you've heard, it isn't the shallow end.

The other thing to be said clearly is that despite our turmoil and some disagreement about who may be a bishop, for the overwhelming majority of parishes in this church, including the one where we sit at this moment, all persons are welcomed and affirmed regardless of their sexuality. For many in this room today, that is good news, but let me add quickly there is risk there, too. There is a cost to liberation from shame, secrecy, and isolation. Persons living in shame, secrecy, and isolation do not have to be good stewards of who they are, do not have to be accountable for how they integrate all the components of their lives into a spiritually healthy whole. Places of shame, secrecy, and isolation are wonderful places to feel sorry for oneself, to escape responsibility and the risk of life.

That is, persons who find themselves suddenly safe to live with *nothing* to hide also find themselves dispossessed of a *place* to hide, dispossessed of a secret world into which they can retreat from the reality of following Jesus all the time, with all their heart, soul, body, and mind. When all of who you are is affirmed, all of you has to come to altar, the parish supper, and the mission. Straight, gay, in between, or undecided, we now find that we are *all* talking about the highest, not the lowest, common denominator, and have the challenge before us to be who we are full-time, and to be that in Jesus Christ.

So with those two thoughts in mind, let me say that in a church without the safety of lots of control, in a church whose Lord dispossesses people of victim status and hiding places, in a church where important authority comes from one's personal integrity much more than from the formal authority of one's office, well, life is not entirely a picnic. Count the cost, Father, there is still time to run.

Not that I expect you to run, but I say all this to make it clear that a man for whom I have developed both respect and affection, and whom I am claiming as a colleague today, is not coming here for a free pass, an easier journey. He is consciously taking on a journey that certainly will affirm him in new ways, but one that will challenge him in others. He will need our prayers; his new colleagues and I promise him our presence, support, and friendship — but there will be only one way, Peter, for you to find out if I am telling the truth, and that is to claim our love, especially when it might be a bit painful to do it.

As my discourse so far reveals, I am a left-brained guy ("not that there's anything wrong with that"). Left-brainedness may be the one characteristic that bishops across the Christian world have in common. This is not irrelevant to my discourse this morning. That left-brained fact about me is why I find a part of my salvation in the *duty* this church places on me to be open to the unexpected, the duty to marvel in the endless variety of God's constant creation, the duty to rest in the joy of knowing that there are indeed many others with many different gifts who complete the tapestry that is the living body of Jesus Christ. It does not come naturally to me; it is a discipline, but it is also a lot easier than my having to make everything come out right for God, as though God needed that. It is a kind of a cross not to be absolutely in charge, to leave at least a *little* room for God to act — but it is worth it, because God does act, and in ways I would never, could never, anticipate, in my tidiness of mind. I say this because I think I am not the only one in the room who needs to remember what it means to be dispossessed of the illusion of control or the much more insidious illusion of tidiness.

What specific cross the form of discipleship he takes on today will lay on Fr. Peter, what new journey he will be asked to travel, is not yet known, and cannot be known at this point. What we do know is what comes in the next chapter in Luke's Gospel. Chapter 15 is Luke's field day. Jesus is criticized for befriending people, in fact for welcoming and even eating with people others found it preferable, even comforting, to reject and never been seen with. Jesus retorts with the parables of the lost coin, lost sheep, and lost son — you know those stories. The point is that to any who will let themselves be befriended today, Jesus reveals the same commitment and hospitality. If Jesus remains available even to the tightly wrapped tax collector and left-brained Cephas-types of the New Testament — how much more is he present for those whose hearts are open, more easily loved and loving, folks like you, my friend and brother? I don't know where today will lead, but I know Christ will be with you in the best and in the worst of it as long as you let him love you, and I ask you to rest in that, as each of us who tries to follow him must learn to do if we are to find any peace and even a measure of joy.

Okay. I almost made it to the end without showing my ignorance, but I find that I can't resist a word about icons, after all: the main thing I know about icons is that they can be windows, and in that respect I know that they do work! To my new colleague I say that this community of sometimes ragtag ecclesial hybrids today asks God that for us you will be what you paint, a window. We ask God that as you speak the word, as you lift the bread and cup among us, God will use the integrity of your soul as a window through which to show us more of the Christ who loves each of us as we are. We ask that in some small way we can be that for you, too. We ask all that believing the ancient words, "he who calls you is faithful — He will do it."